SICILIAN COOKERY

Eufemia Azzolina Pupella

SICILIAN COOKERY

Bread and Pizzas, Appetiters, Pasta, Soup and Rice Dishes, Sauces, Meat, Fish, Desserts and Confectionery

PHOTOGRAPHS BY
PIER SILVIO ONGARO

BONECHI

Editorial conception: CASA EDITRICE BONECHI

Project and production: ANTEPRIMA

Translated by: STEPHANIE JOHNSON

American measurements by: LORA VEZZOSI

Photolitho: LA COMPOSIZIONE

ISBN 88-476-0463-X

The photographs in this book were taken specially by Pier Silvio Ongaro, Agenzia Polis, at the Ristorante
"A cuccagna" in Palermo.
The recipes and photos on pages 146, 152 and 154 belong to the archives of Casa Editrice Bonechi.
Photographer: Andrea Fantauzzo.

A TAVOLA SI SCORDANO LI TRIVULI

(Tribulations are forgotten at the dinner table)

E. Alaimo "Proverbi Siciliani" Edit. Martello

For my children Silvano,
Marco, Massimo,
Mario and Sandra

Why a book of Sicilian recipes? For just over thirty years I have lived with my family in Milan. Many of our friends are not Sicilian and they have always appreciated the dishes prepared for them and many a time have they spurred me on to collect together the recipes for our dishes.

I accordingly decided to collect and select the recipes, all hand-written on faded pages and kept in boxes - some of them quite precious - inherited by my family and that of my husband, almost as if the secret of a gastronomic heritage was to be preserved.

I did not confine myself just to our families' recipes, but the collaboration of friends and relatives who live in different areas of Sicily was also sought.

The material gathered together is vast owing to the variety in the dishes. There are very rich, elaborate recipes which require hours and hours of work, and there are simple recipes which are at the same time nutritious. In fact, there are two types of home cuisine in Sicily: the baronial or "monzu" (Italianised from the French "monsieur" as the cook used to be called) and the daily fare of the people.

The status symbol for the rich and noble was being over-weight; indeed, gout was the disease of the powerful. The peasant, the fisherman and the miner could only afford meat sometimes on Sundays or during the feasting on cel-

alone found use in the kitchen. Sicily's history has, for many centuries, been characterised by the domina-tion of heterogeneous civilisa-tions which have left their mark not only on the territo-ry but on the culinary tradi-

ebration days, religious or otherwise. The longer-living Sicilians belonged to the latter category. I have collected the recipes of the simple folk for two reasons. Theirs is a healthy cuisine, varied and fragrant, being based on vegetables and with-out animal fat. Condiments often have uncooked olive oil as their base. The second reason is that many of these recipes are quite simple to make

tions of the island. Therefore, in the ingredients and in the dishes enriched with the inventiveness of the Sicilians, it is possible to find traces of the different peoples who have followed each other on Sicilian soil. Over time, every domination imported their own seeds and spices.

up, though at the same time fanciful.

It is for this reason that dietologists have, for quite a few years now, recommended this type of cuisine as an example of correct, balanced nutriment, referred to (even abroad) as the "Mediterranean diet". I have purposefully intro-duced two or three recipes of baronial cook-ing as an example of the cuisine used only on important occasions.

The great variety in Sicilian recipes is due to the difficulties in com-munication that existed between one area of Sicily and another. In fact, local products

While carrying out this research, I was fasci-nated to peruse Sicily's course of history and cus-toms through her gas-tronomy. The presence of the Greek civilisation can be seen in the usage of green and black olives, salted ricotta cheese, the Homeric lamb grilled over char-coal, fish, honey and, above all, wine, the production of which was begun by the first Greek colonisers. Going back to the Roman period, when Sicily was considered the granary of Italy, are the "maccu di fave" (mashed broad beans, from the Latin "mac-care"), stuffed cuttle-fish, baked onions sea-soned with oil and vin-egar, sausages and the "sanguinacci" or blood sausages which were always very much appreciated at the sumptuous banquets given at the Villa del Casale in Piazza Armerina.

After the fall of the Roman Empire, Sicily was not spared invasion by Northern peoples (the Franks and the Goths) who, however, did not stay long enough to leave a mark on the culinary art. On the other hand, the Byzantines imported a few spices from the East which continue to be consumed today. From the architectural and cultural points of view, the island recovered all its splendour with the Arabs and flourished once more. Great innovations were also made with regard to the cuisine and dishes became increasingly varied and sophisticated. Thanks to the introduction of the cultivation of sugar cane, refined sugar became the principle ingredient of a good many sweet dishes (such as the "royal paste" or marzipan) and, associated with ricotta and the candied peel of oranges and lemons (it was indeed the Arabs who imported the cultivation of citrus fruit), allowed the famous cassata to be concocted. The use of mulberries, aniseed, sesame and some spices such as cinnamon and saffron goes back precisely to this period. Sorbets were prepared with essences from fruit and flowers and the snow carried down from Mount Etna, and the ice-cream that can still today be found in the Trapani area was made with jasmine oil. The most obvious trace of the encounter with the Arabian civilisation is couscous in the zone around Trapani, differing from the North African dish only in that it is served with a fish soup.

The period of the Norman conquest is responsible for the use of salted cod and salted and smoked herrings. After the incident of the Sicilian Vespers in 1282 and the consequent liberation by the Angevins who had succeeded to the Normans, the Kingdom of Sicily was constituted and it was in this period that the distinction began between the nobles' or baronial cuisine (so-called "monzu"), which had castles and convents as a setting, and popular cooking which developed in taverns and inns. The distinction between these cuisines is often not so obvious because the name of the dish is the same, but the ingredients and how it is served differ.

Following the arrival of the Spaniards, these two types of cuisine continued along parallel tracks, both of them introducing the use of the tomato from America which goes so well with aubergines, onions and sweet peppers, whereas

the wild fennel used in so many recipes originally came from the Canary Islands.

Today, with the facility of commercial exchange and preservation by deep freezing, gastronomic customs have also changed.

We are no longer scandalised if a restaurant in Catania or Palermo includes tagliatelle with a ham-and-cream sauce on the menu. Only the tagliatelle in this dish are truly Sicilian, provided they are fresh and home-made.

Just as ham and cream are used in Sicily, so markets in the North of Italy have the ingredients of Sicilian cuisine, such as wild fennel leaves, capers, oregano and "caciocavallo" cheese. Talking about "caciocavallo", I have found it - just think - in the United States, at Santa Clara in California. My husband and I were staying with friends and, on the occasion of a party in our honour, I thought of preparing "arancini" (rice patties). My American friends escorted me to a supermarket of Italian food. I found "caciocavallo" which often cannot be found in the North of Italy! To this regard, I have indicated a few alternatives for ingredients which are not always easily available in markets and shops.

Thanks

I wish to thank Simona Abriani, who had faith in this book, and the Iten sisters, particularly Marlene, who tracked down the photographer. He is from Verona, but he lives in Sicily and has absorbed a huge amount of "Sicilianness", knowing how to understand and appreciate all the nuances and contradictions of this complex land, which precisely for this reason is so fascinating. I am grateful to Bianca Maria Fumagalli for her very valid critical help and for having transcribed the whole work. I also give thanks to Peppa Anaclerio for her search for old recipes. Finally, I wish to thank all those friends who were "guinea pigs" for the dishes that I had never prepared before and all those who gave me useful advice.

Restaurant proprietors: Francesco Paolo and Carmelo Sammarco

The pastry cook: Anna Sammarco

INDEX

BREAD AND PIZZAS

APPETISERS

PASTA, SOUP AND RICE DISHES

SAUCES

MEAT

FISH

DESSERTS AND CONFECTIONERY

Notes and Suggestion to Readers:

- **Quantities in the recipes are calculated for four to six servings.**

- Metric measurements are given first, followed by imperial and finally those for American readers. I strongly recommend sticking to the same group of measurements throughout the recipe.

- For dishes which require baking or roasting, I have included the terms "moderate oven" = 150°-160°C / 300°-325°F/Gas Mark 2-3 and "hot oven" 180°C-200°C/350°-400°F/Gas Mark 4-6.

- Mention is made of various Italian cheeses. If you cannot find the "genuine article", here is a basic description to help you decide on worthy substitutes:
  Parmesan cheese is the hard, dry cheese known world-wide as a complement to many dishes and needing no introduction here;
  Pecorino is a hard or semi-hard sheep's milk cheese and is available at varying stages of ripening;
  Made from ewe's milk, **ricotta** is soft and fresh, looking rather like cottage cheese;
  Primosale is a fresh, compact cheese;
  Provola is a semi-hard cheese made from buffalo milk, eaten fresh or smoked;
  Provolone is a mild or sharp hard cheese which is usually smoked;
  Caciocavallo is the same kind of cheese as provolone;
  The **caciotta** mentioned in this book is made from ewe's milk in Tuscany and Sardinia and could at a pinch be substituted with gruyère.

- Quantities for herbs are not defined. It depends on personal taste and the intensity of their aroma. Basil loses its fragrance when dried, so doses will be larger than with fresh basil. Oregano is frequently used in Mediterranean cooking. It may be substituted with less pungent marjoram. Wild fennel may be replaced by the leafy tops of bulb fennel.

- Unless specified, use indifferently anchovies preserved in oil or salt.

- Where mention is made of oil, I refer to extra vergine olive oil, which is essential in Sicilian cooking for flavouring dishes. Though ideal for frying as well, other vegetable oils may be used in different climes.

- A vanilla flavouring can be achieved either with a sachet of vanilla powder (about 0.5g / ¼ tsp), a half to one teaspoon of vanilla extract, or in the traditional way by steeping a pod (bean) in liquid; kept in a dry jar, it can be used again.

- 30g (1oz) of fresh brewer's yeast can be substituted with one-and-a-half packets of active dried yeast.

- Tomatoes are easy to peel if you put them in a hot oven for five minutes. Allow the skins to cool. They will wrinkle up and come away easily from the pulp.

British/American Glossary

Aubergine / Eggplant
Bain-marie / Water bath
Baking tin / Baking pan
Bicarbonate of soda / Baking soda
Broad beans / Fava beans
Chick peas / Garbanzos
Courgettes / Zucchini
Cornflour / Cornstarch
Glacé icing / Frosting

Greaseproof paper / Wax paper
Grill / Broil
Hotplate / Griddle
Icing sugar / Confectioner's sugar
Minced meat / Ground meat
Pulses / Legumes
Spring onion / Scallion
Tinned / Canned
Vanilla pod / Vanilla bean

BREAD AND PIZZAS

*T*here is a wide variety of bread in Sicily, both in the making and in the fanciful shape of the loaves. Bread is never lacking even in the poorest homes. It must always be in plentiful supply and if it becomes stale ("*pani duru mantiene la casa*" - bread solves all household problems), it is used in soups, croquettes and stuffings. Fried breadcrumbs, for example, with salty sardines and wild fennel, become a tasty sauce for spaghetti. (With the characteristic Sicilian sense of humour, the poor man's version of this dish has been baptised "*pasta with the sardines still in the sea*" - in fact, among all the ingredients of the famous sardine pasta dish, it is precisely the sardines which are lacking!).

Idioms concerning bread are numerous. In its dramatic force, one of them expresses the most dire poverty:

> "*Si avissi pignateddu, ogghiu e sali,*
> *facissi pani cuttu; Si avissi pani!*"
> (If I had a small saucepan, oil and salt,
> I would cook some bread soup... If I had some bread!)

Other locutions which convey the sacredness of bread are: "*Pani e fami*" and "*Pani e cuteddu*", i.e. Bread [to serve] with hunger, Bread and a knife [to cut it with]. These expressions convey the absolute lack of accompaniments for bread. Before covering it up and leaving to prove, housewives would inscribe a cross on the top of the loaf and kiss it, thus fulfilling a propitious rite which ended with the insertion of the loaf into the hot oven, accompanying the gesture with litanies proposed by the eldest, with all the others joining in to sing the chorus:

> "*Sant'Agostino ogni pane quantu un cufino*
> *Santa Rita beddu di crusta e beddu di muddica*
> *Sant'Isidoro beddu dintra e beddu fora*"
> (St. Augustine make every loaf as large as a cufino*
> St. Rita make the bread fine of crust and fine of crumb
> St. Isidore make the bread fine within and fine without)

Baking day, which usually fell on Friday, was a joyous day ("*Beniditta ch'idda pasta/ca di venniti s'impasta*" - Blessed is the dough prepared on Friday). So as to exploit the hot oven to the utmost, various types of pizza and stuffed "*calzone*" (a Neapolitan savoury roll) were prepared and the bread was eaten just out of the oven, seasoned with oil and/or olives, cheese and what the larder offered, allowing the combinations to spring from the imagination.

(*) The basket of woven palm leaves which was used in the kitchen as a container. By extension, it was considered a symbol of plenteousness.

CALZONE DI RAGUSA
SAVOURY ROLL RAGUSA-STYLE

♦

- 1 KG / 2 LBS LEAVENED BREAD DOUGH
- 1 KG / 2 LBS BONED LAMB
- 3 SMALL ONIONS
- 1 TBSP TOMATO CONCENTRATE
- 125 ML / 4 FL OZ / ½ CUP RED WINE
- 1 EGG YOLK
- SALT
- PEPPER
- OLIVE OIL

♦

PREPARATION TIME: 1 HOUR

FIRST BROWN THE CHOPPED onion in oil in a pan, then add the pieces of lamb. Pour on the wine and let it evaporate. Add the tomato concentrate dissolved in hot water, season with salt and pepper and leave to cook for about 20 minutes. Oil a baking tin or dish and line with half of the leavened dough. Pour the stew over and cover with the other half of the dough, pressing the edges together with your water-moistened fingers. Prick the pie over with a fork and brush with the beaten egg yolk. Bake in a hot oven for 20-30 minutes.

VARIATION: this dish is prepared on Christmas Eve in Caltanisetta, but there the dough is stuffed with fillets of fried salt cod in a tomato and onion sauce. In Messina, on the other hand, the dish is still made on Christmas Eve, but the filling is made of fried pork sausage, slices of fresh pecorino cheese, spring onions and black olives.

CRESPELLE DI RICOTTA E ACCIUGHE

RICOTTA AND ANCHOVY FRITTERS

♦

- 1 KG / 2 LBS / 6½ CUPS FLOUR
- 50 G / 2 OZ / FRESH BREWER'S YEAST
- 500 G / 1 LB RICOTTA CHEESE
- 6-7 ANCHOVY FILLETS
- LARD OR OIL FOR FRYING

♦

PREPARATION TIME: 2½ HOURS

IN A BOWL, mix the flour together with the brewer's yeast dissolved in warm water and season with salt and pepper. Knead the dough, adding more warm water if necessary. When you have obtained a springy paste, cover with a napkin and a woollen cloth and leave for about 2 hours to rise. In the meantime, cut the anchovies up small and put them in a bowl. In another bowl, crush the ricotta with a fork. When the dough has risen, break off a little and, on the palm of your left hand (previously dampened with water), form a shell. In the hollow, put a piece of anchovy and a tablespoon of ricotta. Pull the same dough up to cover the filling and form a ball or an oval. Pour the oil or lard into a deep-sided frying pan and, when hot, arrange the "crespelle" in it with the aid of a spatula. Fry until golden, dry the "crespelle" on kitchen paper and serve hot.

PANE CALDO CONDITO

HOT SEASONED BREAD

◆

- 1 LOAF OF BREAD STRAIGHT OUT OF THE OVEN
- EXTRA-VIRGIN OLIVE OIL
- SALT
- FRESHLY-GROUND PEPPER

◆

PREPARATION TIME: 30 MINUTES

CONNOISSEURS TELL us that bread must not be cut with a knife when still hot from the oven because it would acquire a metallic flavour. It should, instead, be opened up in your fingers or with a length of clean string. Make slits in the crumb of the two halves and season with oil, salt and pepper. Cover with the other half, pressing your fingers down on the crust in order to spread the oil over both surfaces.

VARIATION: the following may be added to the oil, salt and pepper: a pinch of oregano and/or slices of fresh tomato, anchovies, slices of fresh pecorino or fresh caciocavallo cheese, or else pitted green or black olives. The seasoning is left to your imagination and what you have on your shelves. Another variant can be made with left-over bread which is no longer very fresh; slice the bread and soak in a glass of milk. Fry in hot oil and garnish with a slice of primosale cheese and a little piece of anchovy.

PANE CON I FICHI

FIG BREAD

◆

- 500 G / 1 LB / 3 CUPS HARD-GRAINED FLOUR (OR 800 G / 1¾ LBS LEAVENED BREAD DOUGH)
- 25 G / 1 OZ /FRESH BREWER'S YEAST
- 2 TBSP LARD OR OLIVE OIL
- 300 G / ¾ LB DRIED FIGS

◆

PREPARATION TIME: 3 HOURS

WORK THE BREWER'S yeast, two tablespoons of oil, a pinch of salt and some warm water into the flour until you get a smooth dough. Sprinkle with flour, cover with a napkin and a woollen cloth and allow to prove for 2 hours. Cut the figs into pieces and incorporate into the risen dough. Shape as you wish into loaves, place on an oiled baking tray and bake for 30-40 minutes in a hot oven.

VARIATION: instead of figs, you may use raisins or olives or nuts.

21

PIZZA FRITTA
FRIED PIZZA

♦

- 1 KG / 2 LBS LEAVENED BREAD DOUGH
- 300 G / ¾ LB PRIMOSALE OR OTHER FRESH CHEESE
- 2-3 SMALL TENDER ONIONS
- 4 ANCHOVY FILLETS
- SALT
- LARD OR OLIVE OIL

♦

PREPARATION TIME: 30 MINUTES

SFINCIONE DI CALTANISETTA
SICILIAN PIZZA FROM CALTANISETTA

♦

- 1 KG / 2 LBS LEAVENED BREAD DOUGH
- 1 KG / 2 LBS FRESH TOMATOES
- 1 KG / 2 LBS ONIONS
- 150 G / 6 OZ / 1 CUP BLACK OLIVES
- 1 BUNCH OF BASIL
- 5 ANCHOVIES
- 3 CLOVES OF GARLIC
- 150 G / 6 OZ PRIMOSALE CHEESE
- 50 G / 2 OZ / ½ CUP GRATED PECORINO OR PARMESAN CHEESE

♦

PREPARATION TIME: 1 HOUR

WORK THE LARD or olive oil into the leavened dough, divide into six parts and leave to rise again for a couple of hours. Press out the pieces of dough to form little discs which you will fill with a little chopped onion, cheese slices and pieces of anchovy. Fold each disc over onto itself and press the edges well together with your fingers dampened in water. Fry in hot oil.

VARIATION: at Trapani, another type of pizza is made with leavened dough.
Spread the dough over the bottom of an oiled baking tray or dish and brush the surface with oil. Season with salt, pepper, 3 chopped cloves of garlic, oregano and rosemary. Bake for 20 minutes in a hot oven.

SWEAT THE FINELY-SLICED onion in the oil without letting it fry. Skin the tomatoes, remove the seeds and cut into pieces. Season with salt, pepper and chopped basil. Leave to cook for 15-20 minutes. Line an oiled baking dish with the risen dough and trickle over some oil which you will spread with your hand. Make little hollows here and there with your fingers and insert pieces of garlic, black olives and anchovies. Cover with a layer of primosale cut into pieces and smother with the cooked tomato sauce. Sprinkle the grated cheese over and season with a trickle of oil. Bake for 30 minutes in a hot oven.

SFINCIONE DI PALERMO

SICILIAN PIZZA FROM PALERMO

◆

- 500 G / 1 LB LEAVENED BREAD DOUGH
- 500 G / 1 LB FRESH TOMATOES OR 1 TIN (CAN) OF SKINNED TOMATOES
- 100 G / 4 OZ FRESH CACIOCAVALLO OR PROVOLA OR OTHER SAVOURY CHEESE
- 50 G / 2 OZ / ½ CUP GRATED PECORINO OR PARMESAN CHEESE
- 50 G / 2 OZ / ½ CUP DRY BREADCRUMBS
- 4 ANCHOVY FILLETS
- 1 MEDIUM-SIZED ONION
- BUNCH OF CHOPPED PARSLEY
- 125 ML / 4 FL OZ / ½ CUP OF OLIVE OIL
- SALT
- PEPPER

◆

PREPARATION TIME: 2 HOURS

WORK A GLASS of olive oil and the grated cheese into the leavened dough. Leave to prove for about an hour, wrapped in a woollen cloth.

Meanwhile, in a little oil in a frying pan, gently fry the sliced onion, then add the parsley and the skinned tomatoes, cut into pieces. Season with salt and pepper and leave to simmer over low heat for 20 minutes. At this point, add the anchovies cut into pieces and the sliced caciocavallo or other cheese. Mix well and draw off the heat. In an oiled, deep-sided baking tin or dish, spread out the paste to the thickness of about an inch-and-a-quarter. With your fingers, make a few holes in the top, pour over half the sauce and bake in a hot oven. After about 15 minutes, take the tin out, pour in the remaining sauce and dredge with fried breadcrumbs. Trickle over a little oil and replace in the oven for 30 minutes.

SFINCIONE DI PATATE

SICILIAN POTATO PIZZA

- 500 G / 1 LB POTATOES
- 500 G / 1 LB / 3½ CUPS FLOUR
- 100 G / 4 OZ / FRESH BREWER'S YEAST
- 200 G / 8 OZ SALAMI
- 200 G / 8 OZ PRIMOSALE CHEESE
- 50 G / 2 OZ / ½ CUP DRY BREADCRUMBS

PREPARATION TIME: 2½ HOURS

BOIL THE POTATOES IN SALTED WATER, peel and put through a potato ricer. Heap the purée on a pastry board with the flour and add the yeast dissolved in warm water.

Knead well, adding warm water, if necessary, to obtain a smooth mixture. Dust with flour, wrap the dough up in a napkin, cover with a woollen cloth and leave to prove for two hours.

Oil a baking tin or dish and line the bottom with half the dough, pressing it down with your fingers. On top, arrange one layer of sliced salami and one with most of the primosale cheese slices. Cover with the other half of the dough and a few more slices of cheese. Sprinkle some dry breadcrumbs over the top and bake in a hot oven for 20 minutes.

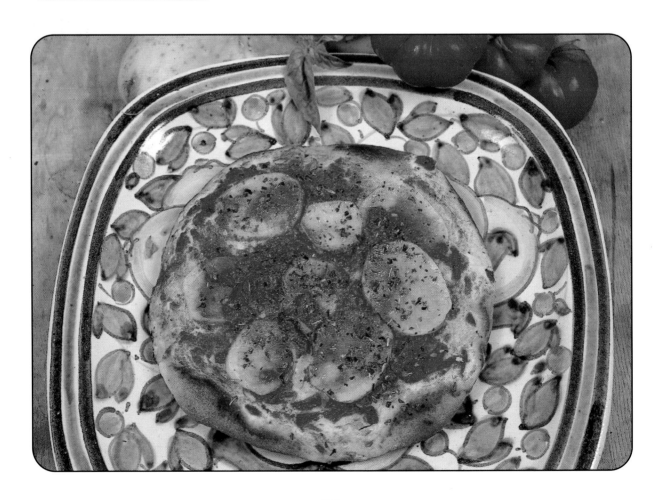

Appetisers

"Cosa licca sa di picca"
(Little things give little satisfaction)

E. Alaimo "Proverbi siciliani" Edit. Martello

Good things must be eaten sparingly
so as not to spoil the appetite.

A starter course did not exist in the old Sicilian cuisine. Many hours before a celebration dinner (whether in the baronial home or that of the common people), the men used to gather together to talk business, sipping wine and nibbling titbits.

Such dishes were based on raw and cooked vegetables: seasoned olives, aubergines (eggplants), courgettes (zucchini) and tomatoes in oil, pickles, salads, timbales and baby omelettes. On the barons' tables, this fare appeared as side dishes to go with the meat and fish or between one course and the next. Whereas in popular kitchens (except on religious feasts and secular holidays), these same dishes were prepared for the main course, after the soups and pasta dishes which were considered of scarce nutritious value.

Included therefore in this chapter are recipes for salads, vegetables, eggs and omelettes.

Omelettes make a very simple dish, quick to get ready, which can solve the problem the hostess faces when she has very little time to come up with a delicious impromptu dinner. The variety is vast and depends on the ingredients lying on the shelves at home and the whim of the cook. Among the wealth of possible recipes, I have chosen two which I find rather unusual and are little known: one with ricotta and one with dry bread crumbs.

CACIOCAVALLO FRITTO CON L'ORIGANO E L'ACETO

FRIED CACIOCAVALLO WITH AN OREGANO AND VINEGAR DRESSING

◆

- 500 G / 1 LB FRESH CACIOCAVALLO CHEESE
- 125 ML / 4 FL OZ / 8 TBSP VINEGAR
- 2 CLOVES OF GARLIC
- OREGANO
- OLIVE OIL

◆

PREPARATION TIME: 30 MINUTES

HEAT A LITTLE OIL IN A FRYING pan with the whole cloves of garlic, which you will remove as soon as they colour. Fry the sliced caciocavallo on both sides, season with salt and pepper and flavour with oregano. Sprinkle the vinegar over and, after a few minutes, turn off the heat.

This dish is eaten at the end of the summer, when shepherds begin to process the cheeses to be ripened.

Fresh caciocavallo can, in fact, only be found at the end of August and the beginning of September.

CAPONATA
AUBERGINE OR EGGPLANT RAGOUT

◆

- **4** AUBERGINES OR EGGPLANTS
- **200** G / **8** OZ / **1 ⅓** CUPS OLIVES
- **50** G / **2** OZ / **¼** CUP CAPERS
- **2** LARGE STICKS OF CELERY
- **1** SOUP LADLE / **4** TBSP HOME-MADE TOMATO SAUCE
- **2** LARGE ONIONS, FINELY-SLICED
- **125** ML / **4** FL OZ / **8** TBSP VINEGAR
- **1** TBSP GRANULATED SUGAR
- A FEW BASIL LEAVES
- OLIVE OIL

◆

PREPARATION TIME: 3 HOURS

DICE THE AUBERGINES and put in a bowl with salted water for about 2 hours. Clean the celery and blanch in salted water for 5 minutes.

Place the capers in a bowl with hot water to draw the salt out and drain after a few minutes. Put the onion in a little oil in a large frying pan, together with the capers and roughly-chopped olives.

Add the sauce, if already made, or else skin four ripe tomatoes, discard the seeds and chop roughly. Stir with a wooden spoon and turn off the heat once a thick sauce has formed. Squeeze the aubergines, dry them carefully and fry in another frying pan.

Fry the celery, cut into small chunks, in the same oil. Put the fried aubergines and celery in the saucepan with the sauce, mix well and blend the flavours for 5 minutes over a low heat. Sprinkle with sugar, pour over the vinegar and, after a few minutes, turn off the heat and cover with the lid. "Caponata" is better served cold in an earthenware bowl and garnished with basil leaves.

CARCIOFI FRITTI IN PASTELLA
BATTER-FRIED ARTICHOKES

- 4 GLOBE ARTICHOKES
- 2 CLOVES OF GARLIC
- 2 EGGS
- 250 G / 8 OZ / 1⅔ CUPS WHITE FLOUR
- 1 LEMON
- 1 SPRIG PARSLEY
- ¼ TSP FRESH BREWER'S YEAST
- OIL FOR FRYING
- OLIVE OIL

PREPARATION TIME: 1½ HOURS

MAKE THE BATTER BY PUTTING the flour in a bowl and blending it into a little warm water (¼ cup). Add the brewer's yeast, allowing to dissolve, then the egg, beaten with a fork, and season with parsley, chopped garlic, salt and pepper. Leave to rest for 30 minutes. Meanwhile, discard the tough and spiky parts of the artichokes and cut into wedges. Blanch in water with the squeezed lemon juice and a pinch of salt for five minutes. Drain, dry, dip them in the batter and fry them in hot oil.

CAVOLFIORE FRITTO IN PASTELLA
CAULIFLOWER FRIED IN BATTER

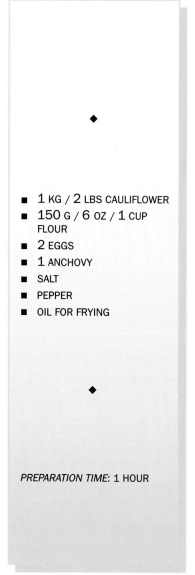

◆

- 1 KG / 2 LBS CAULIFLOWER
- 150 G / 6 OZ / 1 CUP FLOUR
- 2 EGGS
- 1 ANCHOVY
- SALT
- PEPPER
- OIL FOR FRYING

◆

PREPARATION TIME: 1 HOUR

BOIL THE CAULIFLOWER IN SALTED WATER. Drain while still crisp and divide into florets. Make the batter by beating the eggs in a bowl with a fork and sprinkling in the flour, being careful that lumps do not form. Continue to stir briskly, always in the same direction. Add the anchovy, cut into tiny pieces, salt and pepper. Dip the cauliflower into the batter and fry in the hot oil in a frying pan.

FRITTATA CON LA RICOTTA
RICOTTA CHEESE OMELETTE

◆

- 400 G / 14 OZ RICOTTA
- 5 EGGS
- SALT
- PEPPER
- OLIVE OIL

◆

PREPARATION TIME: 30 MINUTES

POUR A LITTLE OIL INTO A FRYING PAN and place in it the ricotta, cut into slices. Brown the cheese on both sides. Beat the eggs with a fork, add salt and pepper and pour onto the ricotta. When the omelette has set on one side, turn it over with the help of the saucepan lid and cook on the other side.

VARIATIONS: follow the same procedure with the addition of grated pecorino cheese and a few leaves of chopped parsley. It was also the usage to beat finely-sliced raw vegetables and aromatic herbs (chopped, tender wild fennel, shallots, asparagus, basil, garlic) together with the eggs, but without the cheese. On the other hand, when other vegetables were used (courgettes or zucchini, potatoes, peas, globe artichokes and cauliflower), they were first boiled and then poured into the beaten egg and cooked in the pan.

GAMBERETTI AL LIMONE
PRAWNS IN LEMON

◆

- 500 G / 1 LB / VERY FRESH, UNCOOKED PRAWNS (SHRIMPS)
- 2-3 LEMONS
- 25 G / 1 OZ / 2 TBSP SALTED CAPERS
- 5-6 MINT LEAVES
- OLIVE OIL, SALT AND PEPPER

◆

PREPARATION TIME: 1 HOUR

SHELL THE UNCOOKED PRAWNS and arrange in a bowl. Squeeze the lemons and pour the juice over the prawns. Season with salt and pepper.

In the meantime, soak the capers so as to eliminate the salt. Drain well and transfer to the bowl with a leaf of mint to lend aroma. Dress with oil.

Leave to macerate, stirring from time to time.

_____

A PIECE OF ADVICE: try getting this dish ready in advance - in the morning, for example, when it is to be relished in the evening. In this way, the prawns will be more flavoursome.

32

INSALATA CON POLPO BOLLITO

BOILED OCTOPUS SALAD

B OIL THE OCTOPUS IN SALTED WATER. When cooked, cut it into pieces and dress with olive oil, salt and lemon to taste.

To help you cook the octopus well without it becoming tough, here is a suggestion from a fisherman: put a wine cork in with the cooking water.

The effect of the cork on the octopus has no scientific explanation, but I can assure you that it *does* work.

♦

- 1 KG / 2 LBS OCTOPUS
- JUICE FROM 1 LEMON
- OLIVE OIL AND SALT

♦

PREPARATION TIME: 1 HOUR

INSALATA FANTASIA DI ARANCE
ORANGE SALAD

♦

- 2 LARGE ORANGES
- SALT
- PEPPER
- OLIVE OIL

♦

PREPARATION TIME: 30 MINUTES

YOU MAY USE two different qualities of oranges for this salad: blood oranges with their red pulp, or the Portuguese ones with their yellow pulp.

Peel the fruit and cut into chunks, dress with oil, salt and pepper. The dish can be enriched with pieces of anchovy or herring and black olives or onion.

Considered an excellent appetiser, this salad stimulates the secretion of gastric juices which prepares the stomach to digest the meal.

VARIATION: you may use lemons instead of oranges. Dress with parsley, chopped garlic, olive oil, salt and pepper.

34

MELANZANE ALLA PARMIGIANA
AUBERGINE / EGGPLANT PIE

♦

- 5 AUBERGINES (EGGPLANTS)
- 1 KG / 2 LBS TOMATOES
- 500 G / 1 LB ONIONS
- 150 G / 6 OZ PRIMOSALE CHEESE
- 100 G / 4 OZ / 1 CUP GRATED CHEESE
- BASIL
- SALT
- PEPPER
- OIL FOR FRYING

♦

PREPARATION TIME: 2 HOURS

PEEL AND SLICE THE AUBERGINES and soak in salted water for about 30 minutes. Drain, rinse, dry and fry in very hot oil.

In the meanwhile, make some tomato sauce with plenty of basil. Put a layer of aubergine in the bottom of an oiled baking pan, cover with the tomato sauce, sprinkle grated cheese over and arrange a few slices of the primosale on top. Continue with more layers of aubergine, dressed as previously, until all the ingredients have been used up.

The final layer will consist of aubergine and grated cheese. Drizzle a little olive oil over and bake in a hot oven for about 15 minutes.

VARIATION: peel the aubergines, slice and soak in salted water for about thirty minutes.
Drain, rinse, dry and place on a scalding hotplate (griddle). Season in the same way as in the recipe above. The vegetable becomes more digestible in this way, and is just as tasty.

MELANZANE RIPIENE
STUFFED AUBERGINES / EGGPLANTS

◆

- 3 AUBERGINES (EGGPLANTS)
- 4 CLOVES OF GARLIC
- 4-5 RIPE TOMATOES
- 100 G / 4 OZ / ¼ LB CACIOCAVALLO OR A SHARP PROVOLA CHEESE
- 50 G / 2 OZ / ½ CUP GRATED CHEESE
- 4 OR 5 BASIL LEAVES
- SALT
- PEPPER

◆

PREPARATION TIME: 1 HOUR

CUT THE AUBERGINES LENGTHWAYS. With the tip of a sharp knife, make several slits in the flesh of the vegetable and scald in salted water for 10 minutes.

Place the cut side face down on a napkin or a kitchen paper towel to drain.

Dry and allow to cool. Cut the garlic and the caciocavallo into pieces and insert into the slits. Aromatise with some basil and cover each aubergine slice with the tomato sauce which you will have prepared as follows: gently fry two whole cloves of garlic (to be subsequently removed) in a little olive oil; chop up 4 or 5 ripe tomatoes, skinned and with their seeds discarded; cook for 5 to 10 minutes, stirring; add salt and pepper and aromatise with chopped basil. Mask the aubergines with the sauce, dust with the grated cheese, drizzle over some oil and bake for 30 minutes in a hot oven at 180° C/350° F/Gas mark 4.

OLIVE CONDITE
DRESSED OLIVES

- 500 G / 1 LB / 3 CUPS GREEN OLIVES
- 2 CLOVES OF GARLIC
- BASIL
- PARSLEY
- HOT RED PEPPERS
- OLIVE OIL
- VINEGAR

PREPARATION TIME: 2 HOURS

CRUSH THE OLIVES and season with the garlic, basil, parsley and hot red peppers, all chopped up together. Fill the jar with olive oil to cover and a few drops of vinegar.

VARIATIONS: the olives can be flavoured with pickles, or else with oregano and garlic covered in oil, or even with a brine solution - 1 l (2 pints / 4 cups) water and 200 g (8 oz / ⅔ cup) salt.

This dish goes very well with a salad of tender Florence fennel and/or tomatoes. It is never lacking from the Sicilian larder in any season of the year so unexpected guests can always be offered an "aperitivo".

OLIVE CON PANGRATTATO FRITTO
FRIED BREADED OLIVES

◆

- **500 G / 1 LB / 3 CUPS** GREEN OLIVES
- **100 G / 4 OZ / 1 CUP** DRY BREADCRUMBS
- **1 CLOVE OF GARLIC**
- **HOT RED PEPPER**
- **OLIVE OIL**
- **VINEGAR**

◆

PREPARATION TIME: 2½ HOURS

BROWN THE BREADCRUMBS in a little oil in a frying pan, stirring continuously. Score the olives, put them in a bowl and season with chopped parsley and garlic.
Add the hot red pepper, olive oil, a squirt of vinegar and the dry breadcrumbs. Mix well and serve.

THIS IS AN EASY appetiser to prepare because, in the Sicilian larder, there is never a lack of olives in brine, dry breadcrumbs, garlic, olive oil and hot red peppers. It is an excellent dish to serve with wine.

PANELLE
FLAT CHICKPEA LOAVES

◆

- **500 G / 1 LB / 3 CUPS** CHICKPEA (GARBANZO) FLOUR
- **WATER**
- **SALT**

◆

PREPARATION TIME: 30 MINUTES

BRING A SAUCEPAN WITH SALTED WATER TO BOIL. When it starts to bubble, sprinkle in the chickpea flour. Keep mixing with a wooden spoon until a rather thick paste forms. Pour onto a pastry board and, with the aid of a pallet knife or spatula, spread it out to make a very thin layer. Then, using the rim of a glass, cut out little, round, flat loaves and fry in hot oil.

CROCCHETTE DI PATATE

POTATO CROQUETTES

- 1 KG / 2 LBS POTATOES
- 3 EGGS
- 50 G / 2 OZ / ½ CUP GRATED CHEESE
- 100 G / 4 OZ / 1 CUP DRY BREADCRUMBS
- CHOPPED PARSLEY

PREPARATION TIME: 2 HOURS

BOIL THE POTATOES in salted water. Peel and put through a vegetable mill to make a purée. Season with the grated cheese, the dry breadcrumbs, the chopped parsley, salt, pepper and the 3 egg yolks. Pour the egg whites into a bowl and put the dry breadcrumbs into another. Mix the purée well and form little fingers.

Dip these into the egg whites (whisked up with a fork) and then the breadcrumbs. Deep fry in hot oil.

CROCCHETTE DI PATATE CON CARNE

POTATO CROQUETTES WITH MEAT

- 1 KG / 2 LBS POTATOES
- 4 EGGS
- 50 G / 2 OZ / ½ CUP GRATED CHEESE
- 100 G / 4 OZ / 1 CUP DRY BREADCRUMBS
- 300 G / ¾ LB MINCED (GROUND) MEAT
- 1 MEDIUM-SIZED ONION
- 125 ML / 4 FL OZ / 8 TBSP WHITE WINE
- HOME-MADE TOMATO
- SAUCE
- CHOPPED PARSLEY

PREPARATION TIME: 2 HOURS

BOIL THE POTATOES in salted water, peel and put through a vegetable mill to mash them.

Season with half the grated cheese and dry breadcrumbs, the parsley, salt, pepper and two egg yolks. Keep the egg whites aside in a bowl. Boil the other eggs until hard. Sauté the chopped onion in a little oil until golden, add the minced meat and the white wine. After a few minutes, add the tomato purée and cook until the meat sauce is dense. Add the grated cheese and the roughly-chopped, hard-boiled eggs to the meat. Make cups with the potato mixture, filling them with a spoonful of the meat sauce.

Cover with the remaining potato mixture to form croquettes which you will dip into the whisked egg whites and then into the dry breadcrumbs. Deep fry in hot oil.

PATATE AL FORNO
POTATOES AU GRATIN

♦

- 1 KG / 2 LBS POTATOES
- 500 G / 1 LB ONIONS
- 4 RIPE TOMATOES
- A FEW PIECES OF CHEESE AND/OR SALAMI SAUSAGE

♦

PREPARATION TIME: 1 HOUR

PEEL THE POTATOES, wash and slice. Oil a baking dish and arrange a layer of potato slices on the bottom. Scatter over a little finely-sliced onion, pieces of cheese and/or salami, and pieces of skinned and seeded tomatoes. Continue layering the ingredients until they are all used up. The last layer will be of tomatoes and basil. Trickle a little olive oil over the top and bake in a hot oven for about 45 minutes.

This makes an excellent accompaniment to meat or cheese served up for supper.

PATATE E RICOTTA IN POLPETTE
POTATO AND RICOTTA CHEESE PATTIES

◆

- 1 KG / 2 LBS POTATOES (THE OLDER THE BETTER)
- 100 G / 4 OZ / 1 CUP GRATED CHEESE
- 100 G / 4 OZ / 1 CUP DRY BREADCRUMBS
- 4 EGGS
- 500 G / 1 LB RICOTTA
- CHOPPED PARSLEY
- NUTMEG
- SALT
- PEPPER
- OIL FOR FRYING

◆

PREPARATION TIME: 1½ HOURS

BOIL THE POTATOES, peel and mash them in a vegetable mill.

Add two eggs, the grated cheese, salt, pepper, chopped parsley and a handful of dry breadcrumbs to thicken the mixture. Mix to amalgamate the ingredients thoroughly. In a bowl, mash the ricotta with a fork, season with salt and a little ground nutmeg. Make little nests with the mixture in your palms, dampened with water, and fill up the hollows with a spoonful of ricotta, sealing with more of the potato mixture to form a ball. Dip each patty first into the beaten egg and then into the breadcrumbs.

Deep fry in hot oil. This dish is typical of spring when ricotta is at its best.

PATATE IN TORTA
POTATO CAKE

♦

- 1 KG / 2 LBS POTATOES
- 1 EGG
- 50 G / 2 OZ / ½ CUP GRATED CHEESE
- 100 G / 4 OZ FRESH CHEESE (PRIMOSALE, CACIOCAVALLO OR PROVOLA)
- 50 G / 2 OZ SALAMI OR
- MORTADELLA
- 50 G / 2 OZ / ½ CUP DRY BREADCRUMBS
- PARSLEY
- BASIL

♦

PREPARATION TIME: 1 HOUR

BOIL THE POTATOES in salted water, peel and put through a vegetable mill to mash them.
Season with the grated cheese, parsley, basil, egg, salt and pepper. If the mixture is too soft, add a handful or so of breadcrumbs.
Oil a baking pan and sprinkle a layer of breadcrumbs over it. Spread half the potato mixture over the bottom of the dish. Arrange the salami and cheese slices on top and cover with the rest of the mash. Bake in a hot oven for about 30 minutes until a crust forms.

VARIATION: various ingredients may be used for the filling. You may use up left-over meat stew, sausages, ricotta cheese, meat sauce left over from a pasta dish and minced with peas, etc.....

PEPERONI ARROSTITI
ROAST SWEET PEPPERS

- 8 SWEET (BELL) PEPPERS
- 4 CLOVES OF GARLIC
- 3 ANCHOVY FILLETS
- 1 LEMON
- CHOPPED BASIL
- SALT
- PEPPER OR HOT RED PEPPER
- OLIVE OIL

PREPARATION TIME: 2 HOURS

BAKE THE PEPPERS in a hot oven until they wrinkle and wilt. Take them out and allow to cool. Discard the stalk, eliminate the seeds completely and peel.

Cut the peppers into strips and arrange them in a bowl into which you will have poured a little olive oil. Crush the anchovy fillets sepa-rately with a fork and add. Season the whole lot with the chopped basil and garlic and the lemon juice. Hot red pepper may be added if you wish.

This is an excellent antipasto which can be prepared during the summer and kept in the larder for two or three months.

PEPERONI RIPIENI DI CARNE
MEAT-STUFFED SWEET PEPPERS

- 6 SWEET (BELL) PEPPERS
- 300 G / ¾ LB MINCED (GROUND) MEAT
- 80 G / 3 OZ / ¾ CUP GRATED CHEESE
- 50 G / 2 OZ / ½ CUP DRY BREADCRUMBS
- 2-3 CHOPPED BASIL LEAVES SPRIG OF PARSLEY
- 1 EGG
- 1 SOUP LADLE / 4 TBSP HOME-MADE TOMATO SAUCE

PREPARATION TIME: 45 MINUTES

WASH THE PEPPERS, dry, and remove the stalk. Mix the minced meat in a bowl with the egg, the grated cheese, the dry breadcrumbs and the chopped parsley and basil. If the mixture is not soft enough, add a little tomato purée. Stuff the peppers and arrange them upright in an ovenproof dish with a little water and olive oil to cover the bottom. Bake in a hot oven for about thirty minutes. Serve hot.

PEPERONI RIPIENI ALLA PALERMITANA
STUFFED PEPPERS, PALERMO-STYLE

- 6 SWEET (BELL) PEPPERS
- 150 G / 6 OZ / 1½ CUPS DRY BREADCRUMBS
- 3 ANCHOVY FILLETS
- 100 G / 4 OZ / 1 CUP GRATED PECORINO CHEESE
- 1 SOUP LADLE / 4 TBSP HOME-MADE TOMATO SAUCE
- 30 G / 1 OZ / 3 TBSP SULTANAS OR RAISINS
- 30 G / 1 OZ / 4 TBSP PINE NUTS
- 150 G / 6 OZ DICED CACIOCAVALLO OR SPICY PROVOLA CHEESE
- 100G / 4 OZ SALAMI, CUT INTO PIECES

PREPARATION TIME: 1½ HOURS

REMOVE THE PEPPER STALKS and discard the seeds. Put the oil and the anchovy fillets (crushing them with a fork) in a frying pan. Add the dry breadcrumbs, the sultanas and pine nuts and gently fry everything, continuously mixing so that lumps do not form. Cool and add the grated cheese, the diced cheese and the salami. Pour in a soup ladle of tomato purée to blend everything together.

Stuff the peppers with the mixture and arrange in a baking dish with a little water and oil so that they do not stick to the bottom. Bake for about 30 minutes in a hot oven.

PEPERONATA
PEPPER RAGOUT

- 1 KG / 2 LBS SWEET (BELL)
- PEPPERS
- 2 CLOVES OF GARLIC
- 4 ANCHOVY FILLETS
- 50 G / 2 OZ / 4 TBSP PICKLED CAPERS
- 500 G / 1 LB TOMATOES
- BASIL
- OLIVE OIL

PREPARATION TIME: 45 MINUTES

PUT A LITTLE OLIVE OIL, the chopped garlic and the anchovies, crushed with a fork, in a saucepan. Remove the seeds from the peppers, shred and place in the pan. Cover with the lid and simmer for 15 minutes. Add the capers, the roughly-chopped, seeded tomatoes and the basil. Cook for a further 15 minutes.

POMODORI SECCATI SOTT'OLIO
DRIED TOMATOES IN OIL

- **500** G / **1** LB DRIED TOMATOES
- **4** CLOVES OF GARLIC
- SPRIG OF BASIL, CHOPPED
- SPRIG OF PARSLEY, CHOPPED
- A FEW ANCHOVY FILLETS
- OREGANO
- VINEGAR
- HOT RED PEPPERS
- OLIVE OIL

PREPARATION TIME: 30 MINUTES

BLANCH THE TOMATOES very briefly in a solution of 1 part vinegar to 3 parts water (1 or 2 minutes will be enough). Dry well on kitchen paper. Arrange a layer of tomatoes in a bowl and dress with pieces of garlic, a pinch of chopped basil and parsley and hot red peppers. Cover with olive oil and a few drops of vinegar. Repeat the layers, finishing with the oil in which the anchovies have been dissolved.

POMODORI SFIZIOSI ALLA PALERMITANA
PALERMO-STYLE TOMATOES

- 6 LARGE TOMATOES
- 150 G / 6 OZ / 1½ CUPS DRY BREADCRUMBS
- 30 G / 1 OZ / 2 TBSP CAPERS
- 30 G / 1 OZ / 3 TBSP PITTED (STONED) GREEN OLIVES
- 4 ANCHOVY FILLETS
- BASIL
- PARSLEY
- SALT
- PEPPER
- OLIVE OIL

PREPARATION TIME: 2½ HOURS

WASH THE TOMATOES, dry and scoop the flesh out into a bowl. Cover the bottom of a frying pan with a little olive oil and the anchovies, crushed with a fork. Add the dry breadcrumbs and, stirring continuously, leave to brown. Turn them into the bowl of tomato pulp, add the chopped parsley and basil and a little oil. Mix well and distribute the mixture among the tomato cases. Arrange in an ovenproof dish and pop into a moderate oven.

UOVA E PISELLI
EGGS WITH PEAS

- 6 EGGS
- 500 G / 1 LB PEAS
- 2 SMALL ONIONS
- SALT
- PEPPER
- OLIVE OIL

PREPARATION TIME: 30 MINUTES

BROWN THE CHOPPED ONION in a saucepan, throw in the peas, season with salt and pepper and add water to cover. Cook for about 15 minutes. Break in the eggs, cover with the lid and lower the flame. When the eggs are veiled in white, draw off the heat and serve.

This is a spring dish when the peas are still small and sweet. They are usually in copious supply and are also used as a sauce for spaghetti.

UOVA SODE IN SALSA DI POMODORO

HARD-BOILED EGGS IN TOMATO SAUCE

◆

- 5 EGGS
- 2 SOUP LADLES / 8 TBSP HOME-MADE TOMATO SAUCE
- 50 G / 2 OZ / ½ CUP DRY BREADCRUMBS
- SALT AND PEPPER
- OLIVE OIL

◆

PREPARATION TIME: 30 MINUTES

BOIL FOUR OF THE EGGS in salted water until hard. Shell, and cut lengthways.

Beat the remaining egg with a fork and plunge each half of the hard-boiled eggs first in the beaten egg and then in the breadcrumbs. Fry in hot oil and embed in the sauce. Cook for five minutes before serving.

THIS DISH was a main course in the daily fare of the common people. As with almost all main course dishes, the sauce can also be exploited served up with pasta for a first course.

48

ZUCCA ALL'AGRODOLCE

SWEET AND SOUR PUMPKIN

- 1 KG / 2 LBS PUMPKIN (SQUASH)
- 1 CLOVE OF GARLIC
- 125 ML / 8 TBSP VINEGAR
- 1 TBSP GRANULATED SUGAR
- PINCH OF CINNAMON
- A FEW MINT LEAVES
- OLIVE OIL

PREPARATION TIME: 1 HOUR

CUT THE PUMPKIN into slices roughly ½ in thick and fry in hot oil with the whole clove of garlic which you will discard as soon as it colours. When all the slices are fried, put them back all together in the pan, draining off the superfluous oil. Dredge with sugar, chopped mint and cinnamon. Mix with care, pour the vinegar over, cover with the lid and turn off the heat.

SICILIAN PUMPKIN (squash) and courgette (zucchini) recipes are rather scarce. The reason is that this vegetable is considered to be insipid. There is a proverb which goes "Sali mitticinni nà visazza / conzala come vuoi è sempre cucuzza". (Add a lot of salt and seasoning because pumpkin it always remains.)

ZUCCHINE FRITTE IN AGRODOLCE

FRIED COURGETTES WITH A SWEET AND SOUR SAUCE

◆

- 1 KG / 2 LBS COURGETTES (ZUCCHINI)
- 125 ML / 4 FL OZ / 8 TBSP VINEGAR
- 1 TSP GRANULATED SUGAR
- 4-5 MINT LEAVES
- 30 G / 1 OZ / 3 TBSP SULTANAS OR RAISINS
- 1 CLOVE OF GARLIC

◆

PREPARATION TIME: 30 MINUTES

SCRAPE THE COURGETTES and slice into rounds. Fry in very hot oil where you will have put the whole clove of garlic, to be removed as soon as it colours. When all the courgettes are fried, put them back into the frying pan and sprinkle with the sugar, chopped mint and sultanas.

Mix carefully and pour over a glass of vinegar. Cover and turn off the heat.

VARIATION: if you add 4/5 beaten eggs with salt and pepper and a pinch of parsley to the fried courgettes, you will obtain an excellent omelette to be cooked in a pan with very little oil.

ZUCCHINE RIPIENE
STUFFED COURGETTES

♦

- 1 KG / 2 LBS COURGETTES (ZUCCHINI)
- 300 G / ¾ LB MINCED (GROUND) MEAT
- 1 MEDIUM-SIZED ONION
- 30 G / 1 OZ / 2 TBSP CAPERS
- 50 G / 2 OZ / ⅓ CUP GREEN OLIVES
- A FEW TABLESPOONS HOME-MADE TOMATO SAUCE
- BASIL
- SALT
- OLIVE OIL

♦

PREPARATION TIME: 1 HOUR

BLANCH THE COURGETTES for 10 minutes. Drain, allow to cool and cut lengthways. With the aid of a teaspoon, scoop out the flesh which you will set aside in a bowl. Place the hollowed-out courgette shells in an oiled baking dish. Put the meat and the chopped onion, capers, olives and basil in the bowl containing the vegetable pulp. A few spoonfuls of tomato purée will bind the mixture better. Mix well, spoon the mixture into the "shells", drizzle a little olive oil over and place in a hot oven for about 30 minutes.

ZUCCHINE SOTT'OLIO
COURGETTES IN OIL

- 1 KG / 2 LBS COURGETTES (ZUCCHINI)
- 4 CLOVES OF GARLIC
- 3 ANCHOVY FILLETS
- A FEW MINT LEAVES
- OREGANO AND HOT RED PEPPER
- OLIVE OIL AND VINEGAR
- SALT

PREPARATION TIME: 30 MINUTES

CUT THE COURGETTES into "julienne" strips and blanch in a saucepan with two parts of salted water and one part of vinegar for 5 minutes.

Drain well and put into a jar or a bowl. Season with pieces of garlic, mint, oregano, hot red pepper, pieces of anchovy and a few drops of vinegar. Cover with olive oil. You may grill the courgettes instead of boiling them, if you like.

COURGETTES IN SICILY are mostly preserved in oil for keeping in the larder. This is an excellent "nibble" and may be used as a side-plate for meat or fish dishes or with hot bread.

PASTA, SOUP AND RICE DISHES

*T*he recipes for pasta and rice dishes (served nowadays as a first course) have been collected all together for reasons of convenience because, in traditional popular Sicilian cuisine, such dishes formed the backbone of their one-course meals.

It would not be correct to speak of "pasta asciutta" (i.e., not in a broth or soup) because liquid sauces containing cooked and raw vegetables were always plentiful and were "soaked up" with bread which was never missing from the table. Only on Sundays and festive days was the sauce enhanced with meat balls, sausages or other meat.

Along coastal areas, the sauce was based on fish, generally tuna, bluefish or seafood (the poor man's meat).

Regarding the alimentation of common folk, dishes in the Sicilian kitchen were prepared according to certain rites. One such rite concerned the draining of pasta: it was to be lifted out of the saucepan with the aid of a long-handled wooden fork and placed on the serving dish. If the accompanying sauce required cheese, then this had to be sprinkled over the pasta before adding the sauce.

Pasta therefore is never really "asciutta" or dry because it is served with the most imaginative sauces, and the cooking water keeps it "gridda" or slithery. The pasta used to be made at home and varied in type depending on the sauce accompanying it.

The names of the dishes, even though adapted to the Sicilian tongue, are reminiscent of their countries of origin. "Tummala" or timbale, for example, seems to derive from the name of the Arab emir Thummel, who lived in Sicily for a long time. The "pasta alla Norma" is a classic dish from Catania in honour of the composer Bellini. Furthermore, in Catania's parlance, "norma" is an adjective qualifying something or someone that is "ne plus ultra". Included among the first course dishes are soups and those based on rice.

Almost no soups in Sicily are watery, certainly not those based on pulses and vegetables. Broth is a thing apart. The type of pasta to be added to the soups is chosen according to the kind of pulse employed. The pasta must be short, cylinder-shaped and ribbed and must be of the correct size to "hold" the pulses. Lentils are generally served with "Ave Marias", beans with "Pater Nosters", chick peas with "attuppateddi". When the broth becomes soup, the "u curadduzzu" are used, i.e. tiny pasta shapes the name of which recalls small, regularly-cut coral stars.

Vegetable soups are (or were) spring and summer dishes. Considered scarcely nutritious, soups were generally enhanced with pork rind, lard, pieces of cheese or marrow bone. Rice was held to be barely nutritious (today it has been revalued) and destined for consumption by the sick and convalescent. There is a proverb which goes:

"Risu mi calu/E nun mi jisu"
(Eating rice prostrates me
and does not boost me up)

E. Alaimo "Proverbi siciliani" Edit. Martello

This consideration is held by the labourer hoeing away who warns that rice does not sufficiently sustain the strength of land workers. Rice dishes are not very numerous and are rather elaborate. The consumption of rice was concentrated around the feast day of Santa Lucia on 13 December. Indeed, the story goes that, in 1636, Sicily had been hit by appalling famine and the production of cereal was not sufficient to feed the population. Legend has it that, because of a violent (though providential) seastorm, a ship laden with rice and wheat was forced to anchor in the port of Syracuse on 12 December. In almost the whole of Sicily, neither bread nor pasta is eaten to honour Santa Lucia, but instead, both sweet and savoury dishes based on corn and rice are consumed - "cuccìa", rice patties, timbales, fritters and rice puddings, etc.

ARANCINE
RICE PATTIES

◆

- 1 KG / 2 LBS / 4 CUPS LONG-GRAIN RICE
- 800 G / 1¾ LBS MINCED (GROUND) MEAT
- 500 G / 1 LB PEAS
- 500 G / 1 LB / 5 CUPS DRIED BREADCRUMBS
- 300 G / ¾ LB FRESH CACIOCAVALLO OR SHARP PROVOLA CHEESE
- 100 G / 4 OZ / 1 CUP GRATED PECORINO OR PARMESAN CHEESE
- 1 MEDIUM ONION
- 7-8 EGGS
- 2 TBSP TOMATO PASTE OR 1 TIN (CAN) TOMATO CONCENTRATE
- 125 ML / 4 FL OZ / ½ CUP DRY WHITE WINE
- BASIL
- OIL FOR FRYING

◆

PREPARATION TIME: 4 HOURS

CHOP THE ONION and sauté in a little oil in a frying pan until golden. Add the meat and stir. Pour in the wine and allow to evaporate. Dilute the tomato concentrate in hot water and add to cover the meat completely.

Season with salt, pepper and basil. Simmer gently for about an hour. Add the peas and continue cooking for about 30 minutes. Stand a colander over a saucepan, pour in the sauce and separate out the solids from the liquid.

Cook the rice in plenty of salted water in a saucepan and drain while still firm (it still has to be fried). Return to the same pan, pour over some of the sauce and stir, adding more if necessary (the rice must be barely coloured).

Add the grated cheese and stir. When cold, add 2 whole eggs and stir. Meanwhile, close at hand, get ready a bowl with the breadcrumbs, a bowl with the diced cheese, a bowl in which to beat the remaining eggs, the saucepan with the rice and a bowl with water to dip your hands into.

Turn some dry breadcrumbs onto large platters which will hold the "arancine" once they are ready.

Take a small quantity of the cooked rice in your right hand and transfer it to your dampened left hand.

Make a shell which you will fill with a little of the meat and peas and 2/3 pieces of cheese.

Close up the patty with some more rice and, still with your hands, shape it into an "orange".

Egg-and-crumb it, compressing it in both hands, and place on the platter with the breadcrumbs. Continue until all the rice is used up. Deep fry in hot oil. To save on oil, I recommend using a not too large, deep-sided pan, frying 3 or 4 patties at a time.

CUSCUS ALLA TRAPANESE
COUSCOUS, TRAPANI-STYLE

◆

- 500 G / 1 LB / 3 CUPS PRE-COOKED COUSCOUS
- 1½ KG / 3 LBS MIXED FISH: E.G. DENTEX OR SEA BASS, GILTHEAD OR SEA BREAM, CUTTLEFISH, CLAMS, GROPER, RED MULLET, MUSSELS, SHELLFISH, ETC.
- 500 G / 1 LB RIPE TOMATOES
- 2 CLOVES OF GARLIC
- 2 STALKS OF CELERY
- 2 CARROTS
- 1 BAY LEAF
- 1 ONION
- 1 SPRIG OF PARSLEY
- 1 SACHET OF POWDERED SAFFRON
- PINCH PAPRIKA
- SALT AND PEPPER
- HOT RED PEPPER

◆

PREPARATION TIME: 4 HOURS

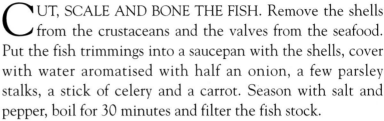

CUT, SCALE AND BONE THE FISH. Remove the shells from the crustaceans and the valves from the seafood. Put the fish trimmings into a saucepan with the shells, cover with water aromatised with half an onion, a few parsley stalks, a stick of celery and a carrot. Season with salt and pepper, boil for 30 minutes and filter the fish stock.

Sauté the remaining half of the onion in oil with a carrot, a stick of celery and some parsley, all chopped up, and the garlic clove left whole for removal as soon as it colours. First add the fish which require a longer cooking time, then the shellfish. Moisten with half of the filtered fish stock, add the tomato pulp and leave to cook for 15 minutes. Add the remaining fish, check the salt and continue cooking for 20 minutes, sprinkling with hot red pepper just before drawing off the heat. Pour the couscous into a large bowl and moisten with a cup of warm water in which you will have dissolved the paprika and saffron. Stir the semolina with your fingers, scooping it up to distribute the water uniformly. Pour the couscous into its special steamer or into a colander with holes on the bottom only, placed over a saucepan half full of water. Before putting on the hob (burner), seal the edges of the pan in contact with the colander with the aid of a cloth previously dampened and rubbed in flour. Wrap this around where the two saucepans meet so that it forms a kind of seal as it cools, which will prevent steam from escaping. Boil for about an hour, stirring the semolina from time to time (it must soak up the moisture, cooking in the steam). Pour the couscous into a roomy bowl, douse with the remaining fish stock and serve with the fish in its sauce.

THE WORD "COUSCOUS" is Arabic in origin and stands to mean little pieces. In fact, couscous consists of tiny lumps of semolina, obtained by working the semolina with rotary movements of the hand (dampened with water) in a special earthenware bowl called "mafaradda". The flour clings together forming tiny grains. The semolina can nowadays be bought already lumped together.

MINESTRA CON LE CASTAGNE
CHESTNUT SOUP

- 500 G / 1 LB DITALINI (SHORT PASTA TUBES)
- 1 KG / 2 LBS CHESTNUTS
- 2 BUNCHES WILD FENNEL LEAVES
- SALT AND PEPPER
- HOT RED PEPPER
- OLIVE OIL

PREPARATION TIME: 1 HOUR

MAKE A HALF-INCH slit on the chestnut skins and blanch them in boiling water for about 10 minutes. Peel and replace in the boiling water with the fennel cut into pieces. When the chestnuts are reduced to a pulp, add the ditalini, salt and hot red pepper and finish off cooking. If necessary, add more boiling water. You should end up with a creamy soup which is not watery. Serve with a trickle of uncooked olive oil.

THIS IS A TIME-HONOURED dish from the mountainous area of the Palermo district. A dear friend from Pollina passed on this recipe.

MINESTRA CON I CECI
CHICKPEA SOUP

- 500 G / 1 LB DITALI (SHORT PASTA TUBES)
- 500 G / 1 LB CHICKPEAS (GARBANZOS)
- 2 SPRING ONIONS/SCALLIONS
- PINCH OF BICARBONATE OF SODA (BAKING SODA)
- A SPRIG OF ROSEMARY
- SALT AND PEPPER
- OLIVE OIL

PREPARATION TIME: 2½ HOURS

SOAK THE CHICKPEAS overnight in water with the bicarbonate of soda. Cook them gently in salted water for about 2 hours, together with the chopped onions and rosemary.

Season with olive oil and pepper and add the pasta previously boiled in salted water. This may be eaten with chunks of stale bread, barely moistened and then fried in hot oil.

PREPARED IN AN EARTHENWARE POT, this is a traditional first course for St Joseph's feast day. It is often enhanced with other pulses (legumes), cooked very simply in boiling water with onion, salt and pepper. As the various pulses have different cooking times, they are only mixed together once cooked and then seasoned with olive oil.

MINESTRA CON IL FORMAGGIO

CHEESE AND TOMATO SOUP

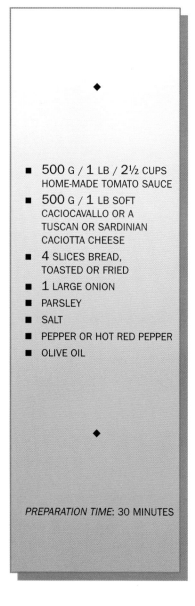

◆

- 500 G / 1 LB / 2½ CUPS HOME-MADE TOMATO SAUCE
- 500 G / 1 LB SOFT CACIOCAVALLO OR A TUSCAN OR SARDINIAN CACIOTTA CHEESE
- 4 SLICES BREAD, TOASTED OR FRIED
- 1 LARGE ONION
- PARSLEY
- SALT
- PEPPER OR HOT RED PEPPER
- OLIVE OIL

◆

PREPARATION TIME: 30 MINUTES

GENTLY FRY THE CHOPPED ONION and parsley in a little oil in a saucepan, adding the tomato sauce, salt, pepper (or hot red pepper) and the caciocavallo cut to pieces. Cook the cheese soup slowly for 15 minutes. Serve with slices of toasted or fried bread.

THIS IS A "BAGNA PANI" SOUP for dipping bread into. Cheese substitutes the traditional fish and the cooking method is the same as for fish soup.

60

MINESTRA CON I FAGIOLI
BEAN AND PASTA SOUP

- 500 G / 1 LB DITALI (SHORT PASTA TUBES)
- 500 G / 1 LB RED KIDNEY OR PINTO BEANS
- 200 G / 8 OZ PORK RIND
- 1 ONION
- PINCH OF BICARBONATE OF SODA (BAKING SODA)
- PEPPER OR HOT RED PEPPER

PREPARATION TIME: 1 HOUR

SOAK THE BEANS OVERNIGHT in water with a pinch of bicarbonate of soda. Sauté the finely-sliced or chopped onion in a little oil, together with the pork rind. Add the beans, drained of the water containing the soda, and cover with hot water. Season with salt and pepper and leave to simmer gently for about 45 minutes. Add hot water and check the salt. When the water boils, pour in the pasta and cook. Dress with uncooked olive oil and hot red pepper.

VARIATION: to give the dish more flavour, add a marrow bone and a tablespoon of home-made tomato sauce during cooking.

MINESTRA CON LE LENTICCHIE
VEGETABLE SOUP WITH LENTILS

- 500 G / 1 LB CONTINENTAL LENTILS
- 400 G / 14 OZ DITALINI OR BROKEN UP SPAGHETTI
- 3 DRIED TOMATOES
- 1 ONION
- A FEW CELERY LEAVES
- SALT
- PEPPER OR HOT RED PEPPER
- OLIVE OIL

PREPARATION TIME: 1½ HOURS

PLACE THE LENTILS in water seasoned with salt and pepper in a pan, adding the chopped onion and the dried tomatoes and celery leaves cut to pieces. Leave to cook for about 1 hour. Boil the pasta separately, or else top up the lentils with hot water, check the salt and throw in the pasta when the water starts to boil. Season with olive oil, pepper or hot red pepper.

61

MINESTRA CON I TENERUMI

PASTA WITH COURGETTE (ZUCCHINI) LEAVES

- **500** G / **1** LB BROKEN UP SPAGHETTI
- **150** G / **6** OZ DICED CACIOCAVALLO OR SHARP PROVALA CHEESE
- **2** BUNCHES OF THE TENDER STALKS AND LEAVES OF COURGETTE (ZUCCHINI) PLANTS OR SWISS CHARD
- **2** RIPE TOMATOES
- **2** CLOVES OF GARLIC
- SALT
- PEPPER
- OLIVE OIL

PREPARATION TIME: 30 MINUTES

CUT THE LEAVES and the tender parts of the stalks up into small pieces, rinse and cook in boiling salted water. After 10-15 minutes, throw in the spaghetti. Gently fry the whole garlic cloves in a little oil in a small saucepan (removing them as soon as they colour) and the tomatoes, skinned and cut into pieces, stripped of their seeds. Cook for about 10 minutes and then pour into the saucepan with the "tenerumi" and the pasta. Before drawing off the heat, add the diced cheese.

MINESTRA D'ORZO
BARLEY SOUP

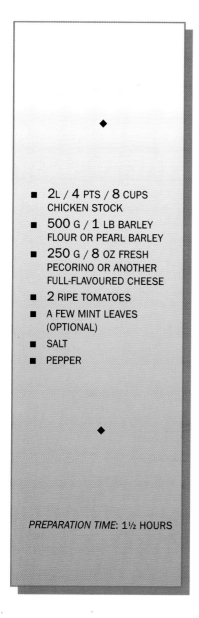

- 2L / 4 PTS / 8 CUPS CHICKEN STOCK
- 500 G / 1 LB BARLEY FLOUR OR PEARL BARLEY
- 250 G / 8 OZ FRESH PECORINO OR ANOTHER FULL-FLAVOURED CHEESE
- 2 RIPE TOMATOES
- A FEW MINT LEAVES (OPTIONAL)
- SALT
- PEPPER

PREPARATION TIME: 1½ HOURS

COOK THE BOILING FOWL in salted water. Remove when cooked.

Add the tomatoes, skinned, seeded and cut into pieces, to the broth.

When the broth comes back to the boil, sprinkle the barley flour over, stirring well to prevent lumps from forming. Cook for 15 minutes over a low flame, add the mint and the diced cheese and draw off the heat. Serve hot. This is a delicate soup which is excellent for children, the elderly and those convalescing.

MINESTRA DI FAVE SECCHE
DRY BROAD BEAN SOUP

◆

- 500 G / 1 LB SHELLED DRY BROAD BEANS
- 2 BUNCHES SWISS CHARD OR SPINACH (ABOUT 400 G /14 OZ)
- 1 MEDIUM-SIZED ONION

◆

PREPARATION TIME: 2 HOURS

SOAK THE DRY BROAD BEANS OVERNIGHT. Cook for an hour in salted water over gentle heat. Drain and mash with a fork. Wash the chard and boil in salted water. While they are cooking, gently sauté the chopped onion in a saucepan, then add the broad beans and the greens, cut up. Season with salt, pepper and uncooked olive oil.

VARIATION: you can add short pasta or broken spaghetti to enrich this dish.

64

MINESTRA DI PATATE

POTATO SOUP

- 500 G / 1 LB DITALINI OR BROKEN UP SPAGHETTI
- 50 G / 2 OZ / 8 TBSP GRATED PECORINO OR PARMESAN CHEESE
- 4-5 LARGE POTATOES
- 2-3 RIPE TOMATOES
- 1 MEDIUM-SIZED ONION
- BASIL
- SALT AND PEPPER

PREPARATION TIME: 30 MINUTES

SAUTÉ THE CHOPPED onion in a little oil, add the potatoes (peeled, washed and diced) and break up the skinned, seeded tomatoes. Season with basil, salt and pepper, cover the potatoes with a cup of hot water and leave to cook for 20-30 minutes. Boil the pasta, drain while still "al dente", dredge with grated cheese and add the potatoes.

MINESTRA DI PATATE, ZUCCHINE E MELANZANE

POTATO, COURGETTE AND AUBERGINE SOUP

- 400 G / 14 OZ DITALINI OR BROKEN UP SPAGHETTI
- 50 G / 2 OZ / 8 TBSP GRATED PECORINO OR PARMESAN CHEESE
- 2 POTATOES
- 2 FRESH TOMATOES
- 1 MEDIUM-SIZED COURGETTE (ZUCCHINI) OR 2-3 SMALL ONES
- 1 AUBERGINE OR EGGPLANT
- A FEW BASIL LEAVES
- OLIVE OIL

PREPARATION TIME: 1 HOUR

CUT UP THE aubergines, potatoes and courgette(s) into chunks. Sauté the chopped onion in a saucepan with a little oil and add the vegetables cut into chunks. Mix well. Throw in the skinned and roughly-chopped tomatoes. Aromatise with basil, season with salt and pepper and add a glass of hot water to cover the vegetables. Cook for about 20 minutes. Check the salt and top up with water (which must always be hot). Throw in the pasta when it boils. Cook until just firm.

ANELLETTI AL FORNO
BAKED PASTA

♦
- 500 G / 1 LB ANELLETTI OR PENNE (UNRIBBED SHORT PASTA)
- 500 G / 1 LB MINCED (GROUND) MEAT
- 400 G / 14 OZ / 2 CUPS SHELLED PEAS
- 100 G / 4 OZ / 1 CUP GRATED PECORINO OR PARMESAN CHEESE
- 300 G / ¾ LB PRIMOSALE OR FRESH CHEESE
- 1 TBSP TOMATO EXTRACT OR A TIN (CAN) TOMATO CONCENTRATE
- 1 MEDIUM-SIZED ONION
- 125 ML / 8 TBSP DRY WHITE WINE
- BASIL
- SALT AND PEPPER

♦

PREPARATION TIME: 3 HOURS

Sauté THE CHOPPED ONION in a little oil in a large saucepan and add the minced meat. Stir and pour in the wine after a few minutes, allowing to evaporate. Then add the tomato extract dissolved in hot water or the tomato concentrate. After half-an-hour over the flame, add the peas and leave to cook a further 20 minutes. Filter and set the liquid aside. Cook the pasta in boiling salted water and drain while still quite "al dente". Pour the pasta back into its saucepan and pour in a little of the sauce and the grated cheese. Oil a baking tin or dish, sprinkle dry breadcrumbs over and make a layer of pasta on the bottom. Cover with some of the meat sauce and slices of primosale cheese. Continue layering the ingredients until they have all been used up. Bake in a hot oven for about 20 minutes.

THE OLD RECIPE used a "ragù" which was not made up using raw minced meat but cooked chunks of meat (beef and pork) which were then chopped up with the aid of a "mezzaluna" knife.

PASTA ALLA NORMA
SPAGHETTI WITH AUBERGINE AND TOMATO SAUCE

◆

- 500 G / 1 LB SPAGHETTI
- 1 KG / 2 LBS RIPE TOMATOES
- 200 G / 8 OZ / 2 GENEROUS CUPS GRATED SALTED RICOTTA CHEESE
- 3 AUBERGINES (EGGPLANTS)
- 3 CLOVES OF GARLIC
- 2 MEDIUM-SIZED ONIONS
- PLENTY OF BASIL
- OLIVE OIL
- SALT
- PEPPER

◆

PREPARATION TIME: 1 HOUR

SLICE THE AUBERGINES and put them in a bowl with salted water for about an hour. Prepare the tomato sauce in the meantime: put the roughly-chopped tomatoes and onion, the whole garlic and the basil in a saucepan. Season with salt and simmer gently until all the liquid has evaporated. Rub the sauce through a sieve or food mill and dress with uncooked olive oil. Remove the aubergines from their soaking water, squeeze and dry them and fry in some hot oil in a frying pan. Boil the spaghetti in plenty of salted water. As soon as cooked to the "al dente" stage, remove from the pan with a long-handled fork, drain and arrange on a serving platter.

Sprinkle half the grated ricotta over and cover with the tomato sauce.

Stir well, garnish with fresh basil leaves and with four aubergine slices.

Serve at table. Each diner will add, to his taste, some more salted ricotta, pepper and fried aubergine.

PASTA CON I CARCIOFI

PASTA WITH ARTICHOKES

- 500 G / 1 LB SPAGHETTI
- 200 G / 8 OZ FRESH PECORINO OR ANOTHER TYPE OF FRESH CHEESE
- 100 G / 4 OZ / 1 CUP GRATED PECORINO OR PARMESAN CHEESE
- 5 TENDER GLOBE ARTICHOKES
- 2 CLOVES OF GARLIC
- 125 ML / 8 TBSP WHITE WINE
- PARSLEY

PREPARATION TIME: 45 MINUTES

CLEAN THE ARTICHOKES, removing the tough outer leaves. Cut across into strips and soak in water into which you have squeezed half a lemon. Sauté the garlic in a little oil in a casserole, add the artichokes, stir and pour on the white wine.

When it has evaporated, add a glass of hot water and cook the vegetables for about 10 minutes. Add the chopped parsley before drawing off the heat.

Cook the spaghetti until "al dente" and drain. Return to the same pan and sprinkle the grated cheese over with half the artichokes.

Oil a baking dish and pour in half the spaghetti. Dredge with pieces of fresh cheese and the remaining artichokes. Cover with the rest of the spaghetti, sprinkle with grated cheese and bake in a hot oven for 15 minutes.

PASTA CON IL CAVOLFIORE
CAULIFLOWER WITH PASTA AND CHEESE SAUCE

◆

- 500 G / 1 LB BUCATINI (PASTA STRAWS)
- 1 KG / 2 LBS CAULIFLOWER
- 100G / 4 OZ / 1 CUP GRATED CACIOCAVALLO, PECORINO OR PARMESAN CHEESE
- 25 G / 1 OZ / 4 TBSP PINE-NUTS
- 50 G / 2 OZ / ⅓ CUP RAISINS
- 4-5 ANCHOVY FILLETS
- ¼ TSP SAFFRON
- 1 LARGE ONION
- SALT AND PEPPER
- OLIVE OIL

◆

PREPARATION TIME: 45 MINUTES

DISCARD THE CENTRAL CORE of the cauliflower and boil the vegetable in salted water. Drain while still firm, reserving the cooking water. Put the anchovies, olive oil and chopped onion in a large frying pan and sauté gently, crushing the anchovies with a wooden spoon. Add the raisins, pine-nuts and the boiled cauliflower florets. Cook for about 10 minutes, mashing the cauliflower to blend in the flavours. In the cauliflower cooking water, boil the pasta until "al dente". Just before turning off the heat, dissolve the saffron in the water. Remove the pasta from the saucepan with the aid of a long-handled fork and place in the saucepan with the cauliflower. Dress with the grated cheese. Mix well and serve.

VARIATION: mix the pasta with half of the cauliflower and arrange in an oiled baking dish. Add the rest of the sauce, sprinkle all the grated cheese on top and trickle a stream of olive oil over. Bake in a hot oven for 15 minutes until a golden crust has formed.

PASTA CON IL CAVOLFIORE E LA RICOTTA

PASTA WITH CAULIFLOWER AND RICOTTA

♦

- 500 G / 1 LB DITALI
  OR BUCATINI
  (SHORT PASTA TUBES)
- 1 KG / 2 LBS CAULIFLOWER
- 500 G / 1 LB / 2¾ CUPS
  RICOTTA CHEESE
- 2 EGGS
- 100 G / 4 OZ / 1 CUP
  GRATED PECORINO OR
  PARMESAN CHEESE
- SALT, PEPPER, OIL

♦

PREPARATION TIME: 45 MINUTES

BOIL THE CAULIFLOWER AND DRAIN, keeping the cooking water. Gently fry the cauliflower in a little oil in a frying pan. Reserve a little of the cauliflower cooking water to soften the ricotta in, mashing it with the aid of a fork. Boil the pasta in the rest of the water, check the salt, drain while still firm and pour into the bowl with the ricotta. Stir well and add a little freshly-ground pepper.

Oil a baking dish and arrange alternate layers of pasta and of cauliflower until the ingredients are used up (you may get two or three layers). Beat the eggs with the grated cheese and pour over the top layer. Bake in a hot oven until a golden crust forms.

PASTA CON IL PESTO ALLA TRAPANESE
TRAPANI PASTA WITH "PESTO"

- 500 G / 1 LB SPAGHETTI
- 500 G / 1 LB RIPE TOMATOES
- 1 OR 2 CLOVES OF GARLIC
- 10 BASIL LEAVES
- 100 G / 4 OZ / 1 CUP GRATED PECORINO CHEESE
- 30 G / 1 OZ / ¼ CUP FRESH OR DRY, CHOPPED, SKINNED ALMONDS
- SALT AND PEPPER
- OLIVE OIL

PREPARATION TIME: 30 MINUTES

POUND THE GARLIC in a mortar together with the basil, almonds and a little olive oil (nowadays an electric blender can be used).

Transfer to a bowl and stir, adding a little olive oil and the grated pecorino.

Skin the tomatoes, discard their seeds, chop roughly and add the garlic and basil. Mix well and leave to rest.

Meanwhile, cook the spaghetti in plenty of salted water, drain while "al dente" and turn into the sauce bowl. Mix well and serve.

THIS USED to be a summer dish to eat while the almonds were still very tender.

PASTA CON IL POMODORO CRUDO PICCANTE

SPAGHETTI WITH UNCOOKED, PIQUANT TOMATO SAUCE

- 500 G / 1 LB SPAGHETTI
- 100 G / 4 OZ / 1 CUP GRATED PECORINO OR PARMESAN CHEESE
- 6 RIPE TOMATOES
- 4 CLOVES OF GARLIC
- SPRIG OF PARSLEY, CHOPPED
- HOT RED PEPPER

PREPARATION TIME: 1 HOUR

CUT UP THE SKINNED and seeded tomatoes in a bowl and add the garlic, pounded or chopped up with the parsley. Season with salt, hot red pepper and olive oil. Leave to steep for about 45 minutes. Boil the spaghetti in salted water, drain while "al dente" and arrange over the sauce.

Stir and serve with grated cheese apart.

PASTA CON LA BOTTARGA

PASTA WITH TUNA ROES

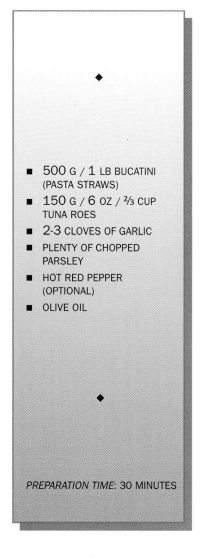

- 500 G / 1 LB BUCATINI (PASTA STRAWS)
- 150 G / 6 OZ / ⅔ CUP TUNA ROES
- 2-3 CLOVES OF GARLIC
- PLENTY OF CHOPPED PARSLEY
- HOT RED PEPPER (OPTIONAL)
- OLIVE OIL

PREPARATION TIME: 30 MINUTES

POUR A LITTLE OIL into a saucepan and gently sauté the chopped garlic and the roes, cut into pieces.

Stir and crush the roes with a fork to blend them in.

Remove from the heat and add the chopped parsley. Boil the bucatini in plenty of lightly-salted water. With the aid of a long-handled fork, turn it into a bowl and add the sauce. Mix well and serve.

Pass some botargo (tuna roe relish) round the table for grating over each plate.

73

PASTA CON LE SARDE
PASTA WITH SARDINES

◆
- 1 KG / 2 LBS BUCATINI (PASTA STRAWS)
- 1 KG / 2 LBS FRESH SARDINES
- 500 G / 1 LB WILD MOUNTAIN FENNEL LEAVES
- 5-6 ANCHOVY FILLETS
- 50 G / 2 OZ / ⅔ CUP CHOPPED TOASTED ALMONDS
- 35 G / 1 OZ / 3 TBSP SULTANAS OR RAISINS
- 35 G / 1 OZ / 4 TBSP PINE-NUTS
- 1 MEDIUM-SIZED ONION
- PINCH OF POWDERED SAFFRON
- WHITE FLOUR
- SALT AND PEPPER
◆

PREPARATION TIME: 3 HOURS

CLEAN THE FENNEL LEAVES and boil in salted water. Drain and reserve the cooking water for boiling the pasta in. Clean the sardines, removing the head and backbone, opening them out flat. In a wide, deep-sided pan, sauté the chopped onion with the anchovies, crushing them with a fork until they dissolve. Add the sultanas, pine-nuts and a pinch of saffron, throw in the chopped fennel leaves, half the sardines and season with ground black pepper.

Cook over gentle heat, stirring from time to time until the sauce has a fair consistency.

Top up the fennel cooking water to boil the bucatini, checking the salt first.

When the pasta is cooked, add a pinch of saffron to the water. Drain and mix the pasta with two parts of the sauce. Turn into a baking tin or dish which has been oiled and crumbed.

Heat the remaining sauce, adding a little oil and the other half of the sardines. Cover the pasta with this sauce.

Scatter over the chopped, toasted almonds. Bake in a hot oven for about 10 minutes to blend the flavours.

VARIATION: you may add all the sardine sauce to the pasta without baking it. Leave a few sardines aside (about ten) to be dipped in flour and fried. Use to garnish the serving dish and then distribute them among all the dinner plates. This is the island's most famous pasta dish.

PASTA CON RAGÙ DELLA FESTA

MACARONI WITH SPECIAL MEAT SAUCE

◆

- 500 G / 1 LB HOME-MADE MACARONI OR RIGATONI
- 500 G / 1 LB FALSOMAGRO OR STUFFED MEAT ROLL
- 500 G / 1 LB POTATOES
- 500 G / 1 LB PEAS
- 3-4 MEAT BALLS PER HEAD
- 2 SAUSAGES (ABOUT 80 G /3 OZ EACH) PER HEAD
- 2 MEDIUM-SIZED ONIONS
- 2 BAY LEAVES
- 1 TBSP TOMATO CONCENTRATE
- SPRIG OF PARSLEY
- SPRIG OF BASIL
- 1 TBSP LARD OR 2 TBSP OLIVE OIL
- 1 MARROW BONE
- 125 ML / 8 TBSP RED WINE
- SALT
- PEPPER

◆

PREPARATION TIME: 3 HOURS

SAUTÉ THE CHOPPED ONION in a little oil in a large, preferably earthenware saucepan. Add the parsley, the bay leaves, the tomato concentrate dissolved in hot water, and the bone with its marrow. Simmer for about 20 minutes. Heat the lard or oil in another saucepan and brown the "falsomagro", the meat balls, the sausages and the potatoes cut into small chunks. Put the rolled meat in the saucepan with the tomato sauce and cook for about 30 minutes. Add the sausages and, after 20 minutes, throw in the potatoes (careful not to overcook) and add the peas. Remove the potatoes first of all from the sauce and put aside, then the sausage and the "falsamagro", which you will leave to cool before slipping off the string and slicing. Arrange the meat slices in the centre of a large serving dish and align the sausages and meat balls to form a crown, with the potatoes forming the outermost ring. Pour some of the sauce with the peas over the "falsomagro" slices. Keep the platter hot in the oven or over a saucepan of hot water for serving as the second course.

Meanwhile, cook the home-made macaroni (or rigatoni), drain when "al dente", arrange on a serving dish, pour the sauce with the peas over and serve immediately.

PASTA CON VONGOLE FRESCHE
SPAGHETTI WITH FRESH CLAMS

- ■ 500 G / 1 LB SPAGHETTI
- ■ 500 G / 1 LB / 2 GENEROUS CUPS SHELLED BABY CLAMS
- ■ 4 ANCHOVY FILLETS
- ■ 2 CLOVES OF GARLIC
- ■ SPRIG OF PARSLEY
- ■ 125 ML / 4 FL OZ / ½ CUP DRY WHITE WINE
- ■ SALT
- ■ PEPPER OR HOT RED PEPPER
- ■ OLIVE OIL

PREPARATION TIME: 30 MINUTES

SAUTÉ THE GARLIC, chopped, in some oil in a saucepan, together with the anchovies, crushed with a fork. Add the clams and cook for about 10 minutes. Sprinkle over the wine. Once evaporated, add the parsley, the pepper or hot red pepper and turn off the heat. Boil the spaghetti in plenty of salted water, drain while still "al dente", turn into a serving bowl and serve with the sauce.

VARIATION: 500 g (1 lb) ripe tomatoes, skinned, seeded and roughly-chopped, may be added after the wine has evaporated. They must cook for at least 5 minutes. Never serve cheese with clams.

PASTA CON VONGOLE E COZZE
SPAGHETTI WITH CLAMS AND MUSSELS

- ■ 500 G / 1 LB SPAGHETTI
- ■ 500 G / 1 LB BABY CLAMS IN THEIR SHELLS
- ■ 500 G / 1 LB MUSSELS IN THEIR SHELLS
- ■ 3 CLOVES OF GARLIC, CHOPPED
- ■ SPRIG OF PARSLEY, CHOPPED
- ■ HOT RED PEPPER

PREPARATION TIME: 1 HOUR

WASH THE MUSSELS and clams thoroughly under running water. Put a little water in a saucepan, bring to the boil and throw in the shellfish. Cook until the shells have opened, then take them out, reserving their liquor. Remove the flesh from the shells, leaving a dozen or so intact for decorating the serving dish with. Sauté the garlic in a frying pan (better if it is an earthenware pot), add the shellfish, season with salt and pepper and cook for 15 minutes. Just before turning off the heat, add the chopped parsley. Boil the spaghetti in the shellfish cooking water, drain while still "al dente" and transfer to the frying pan or earthenware pot. Stir well and serve in a terracotta bowl. Garnish with the clams and mussels that you have put aside and serve the hot red pepper separately for those who like it.

PASTA CON ZUCCHINE FRITTE
SPAGHETTI WITH FRIED COURGETTES

- 500 G / 1 LB SPAGHETTI
- 4 COURGETTES (ZUCCHINI)
- 2 CLOVES OF GARLIC
- GRATED PECORINO OR PARMESAN CHEESE
- SALT
- PEPPER
- OLIVE OIL

PREPARATION TIME: 45 MINUTES

CUT THE COURGETTES into rings and fry in hot oil which has been flavoured with 2 cloves of garlic, removed when golden. Boil the spaghetti, drain while still resistant to the tooth and turn into a bowl.

Dress with the courgettes and the frying oil. Pass pepper and some grated cheese round separately.

This is a classic summer dish, especially in the Palermo area.

77

TIMBALLO DI RISO
RICE TIMBALE

- 1 KG / 2 LBS / 4 CUPS LONG-GRAIN RICE
- 600 G / 1½ LB MINCED (GROUND) MEAT
- 500 G / 1 LB / 2¼ CUPS SHELLED PEAS
- 200 G / 8 OZ PRIMOSALE CHEESE
- 150 G / 6 OZ / 1½ CUPS GRATED CACIOCAVALLO OR PARMESAN CHEESE
- 2 EGGS
- 2 ONIONS
- 2 CLOVES OF GARLIC
- 1 SMALL TIN (CAN) TOMATO CONCENTRATE
- 1 GENEROUS TBSP TOMATO PASTE
- 125 ML / 4 FL OZ / ½ CUP DRY WHITE WINE
- SALAMI
- BASIL
- CINNAMON AND GRANULATED SUGAR

PREPARATION TIME: 1½ HOURS

BROWN THE CHOPPED ONION and the whole garlic (to be removed as soon as it colours). Add the minced meat, stir and pour the white wine on after a few minutes. Allow to evaporate and pour in the tomato concentrate, dissolved in a cup of hot water. Add the salt and pepper and aromatise with the chopped basil. Cook for about 30 minutes. Add the peas and continue cooking for about 15 minutes. Meanwhile, cook the rice in salted water and drain while still firm. Fill a small bowl with plain rice and set aside. Dress the rice with two thirds of the grated cheese and the tomato sauce. Arrange half of the rice in an oiled baking tin or ovenproof dish and place slices of primosale and salami on top. Cover with the other half of the rice. Beat the egg with the rest of the caciocavallo, a pinch of cinnamon and a teaspoon of sugar. Pour the mixture into the bowl of plain rice, stir and pour onto the timbale to make the final layer. Bake in a hot oven for about 20 minutes. The name derives from Thummel, the Arab emir who lived in Sicily for a long time.

TIMBALLO DI RISO CON LE MELANZANE
RICE TIMBALE WITH AUBERGINES

- 500 G / 1 LB / 2 CUPS LONG-GRAIN RICE
- 1 KG / 2 LBS RIPE TOMATOES
- 150 G / 6 OZ PRIMOSALE CHEESE
- 50 G / 2 OZ PECORINO CHEESE
- 4 AUBERGINES (EGGPLANTS)
- 1 ONION
- POWDERED SAFFRON
- BASIL AND PARSLEY

PREPARATION TIME: 2 HOURS

SLICE THE AUBERGINES and put to soak for an hour in salted water. Squeeze them, dry in kitchen paper and fry in hot oil. Sauté the chopped onion in a saucepan, skin the tomatoes, discard their seeds and roughly chop. Add the onion with the chopped basil and parsley, season with salt and pepper and cook gently for about 30 minutes. Boil the rice in salted water and dissolve a pinch of saffron powder in it. Oil a baking dish, make a layer of rice and cover it with the sauce, the fried aubergines and a few slices of primosale. Repeat the layers until all the ingredients have been used up. Dredge with grated pecorino cheese and bake in the oven for 20 minutes. Before serving, sprinkle with chopped basil and parsley.

SAUCES

"Nun c'è megghiu sarsa di la fami"
(There is no better sauce than hunger)

E. Alaimo "Proverbi Siciliani" Edit. Martello

The sauces for serving with pasta are described in all the recipes in the chapter on pasta dishes. I wish here to repeat the simplest recipe for fresh tomato sauce that forms the core for a great number of dishes. Prepared in the summer, this sauce is preserved in glass jars to be consumed during the winter.

The sauces presented in this chapter are condiments for boiled or grilled meat and fish. In the daily fare of the common folk, sauces were not contemplated for boiled meat and fish dishes - the only dressing was olive oil and lemon or pickles. I have chosen to give the recipes for sauces used in the "monsù" cuisine where the ability in preparing them can be expressed. Indeed, it was the French who introduced their sauces based on olive oil, garlic, lemon and oregano and, in the more sophisticated dishes, almonds, pine-nuts, olives, capers, etc. These sauces are quick and simple to make and enhance dishes with their colour and flavour.

Once you begin to make them, your guests will show immense gratitude.

AGLIATA
GARLIC SAUCE

◆

- 4-5 CLOVES OF GARLIC
- 125 ML / 4 FL OZ / ½ CUP OF WHITE WINE VINEGAR
- OLIVE OIL

◆

PREPARATION TIME: 5 MINUTES

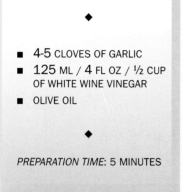

SAUTÉ THE GARLIC (broken into two or three pieces or else chopped) in hot oil in a little pan. Pour in the vinegar, allow to evaporate for 2 minutes and draw off the heat. This sauce is particularly suitable with fried blue-fish.

SALSA DI CIPOLLA CON L'ACETO
ONION AND VINEGAR SAUCE

◆

- 1 ONION
- 60 ML / 2 FL OZ / ¼ CUP VINEGAR
- PARSLEY
- SALT AND PEPPER
- OLIVE OIL

◆

PREPARATION TIME: 15 MINUTES

CHOP THE ONION and sweat in a little oil without frying. Add half a glass of hot water. When it has evaporated, sprinkle the vinegar over. Give this 2-3 minutes to evaporate and pour the sauce over tuna fish or fried salted cod.

81

SALSA DI MANDORLE
ALMOND SAUCE

- 1 LARGE ONION
- 25 G / 1 OZ / 2½ TBSP GREEN OLIVES
- 10 G / 1 OZ / 2 TBSP CAPERS
- 2 RIPE TOMATOES
- 2 ANCHOVY FILLETS
- 25 G / 1 OZ / 4 TBSP CHOPPED AND TOASTED ALMONDS
- 25G / 1 OZ / 2 TBSP GRANULATED SUGAR
- 25 G / 1 OZ / 3 TBSP WHITE FLOUR
- 60 ML / 2 FL OZ / ¼ CUP VINEGAR

PREPARATION TIME: 30 MINUTES

I N A LITTLE OLIVE OIL in an earthenware pot, brown the roughly-chopped onions, the anchovies broken into little pieces, the flour and the almonds, olives and capers chopped up together, along with the skinned, seeded and roughly-chopped tomatoes. Stir and cook for 10 minutes. Before turning off the heat, sprinkle with sugar and vinegar and allow to evaporate for 2 or 3 minutes.

This sauce is excellent served with boiled fish.

SALSA DI MENTA
MINT SAUCE

- 60 ML / 2 FL OZ / ¼ CUP VINEGAR
- SALT
- PEPPER
- OLIVE OIL

PREPARATION TIME: 15 MINUTES

P UT THE OIL, vinegar, salt and pepper in a little bowl. Blend well with a fork and add the finely-chopped mint. Stir well and serve this sauce with boiled meat.

SALSA DI SEMI DI PAPAVERO
POPPY SEED SAUCE

- 100 G / 4 OZ / 1 CUP TOASTED ALMONDS
- 50 G / 2 OZ / ½ CUP DRY BREADCRUMBS
- 2 CLOVES OF GARLIC
- 15 G / ½ OZ / 1 TSP POPPY SEEDS
- 1 BOILED POTATO
- 1 SPRIG PARSLEY, CHOPPED
- 60 ML / 2 FL OZ / ¼ CUP VINEGAR
- HOT RED PEPPER
- OLIVE OIL AND SALT

PREPARATION TIME: 20 MINUTES

POUND THE GARLIC, almonds, parsley, poppy seeds and the potato in a mortar (today an electric chopper or food processor can be used).

Transfer to a bowl and add the oil, alternated with the vinegar, stirring all the time, until the sauce becomes soft and thick. Excellent for boiled meat and fish.

SALSA DI POMODORO
HOME-MADE TOMATO SAUCE

- 1 KG RIPE TOMATOES
- 2 LARGE ONIONS
- 5-6 BASIL LEAVES
- SALT
- PEPPER OR HOT RED PEPPER
- OLIVE OIL

PREPARATION TIME: 15 MINUTES

PLACE THE ROUGHLY-CHOPPED TOMATOES and onions in a saucepan and add the basil and salt. Cook for 30 minutes. Put through a "mouli lègumes" (food mill) and season with uncooked olive oil and pepper or hot red pepper.

THIS SAUCE is the basic one which we used to make in my family not just for serving over spaghetti or other types of pasta, but also for masking excellent main dishes such as meat balls, stuffed vegetables, egg dishes, etc. There are various variations to this sauce: it can be made by first frying the onion and/or garlic, or else with herbs and the most imaginative condiments. Furthermore, it varies from family to family. Indeed, to take away the acidity of the tomatoes, some families add bicarbonate of soda and others sugar. In any case, tomato sauce is the sauce par excellence.

SALSA MARINARA
FISH SAUCE

◆

- 500 G / 1 LB FISH TRIMMINGS: BONES AND HEADS
- 25 G / 1 OZ / 3 TBSP WHITE FLOUR
- PARSLEY SPRIG
- BAY LEAF
- 1 LEMON
- 2 EGG YOLKS
- 125 ML / 4 FL OZ / ½ CUP WHITE WINE
- 1 ONION
- FEW THYME LEAVES
- SALT AND PEPPER

◆

PREPARATION TIME: 1 HOUR

WASH THE FISH TRIMMINGS and cook for 30 minutes in a saucepan with water, parsley stalks, half the onion, the bay leaf, thyme, half the wine and salt. Filter the stock and keep hot over gentle heat. Chop the remaining onion which you will sauté in a pan with the oil, adding the flour and stirring with a wooden spoon. Pour over the remaining wine and leave to evaporate before adding the hot fish stock. Cook for 15 minutes, stirring constantly. Sprinkle over the parsley, two beaten egg yolks and lemon juice and draw off the heat. This sauce is excellent with boiled fish.

HERE IS A SAUCE concocted with what usually gets thrown away - the fish heads and bones (cleaned before being cooked). The aristocracy appreciated their own monsu's brand of micro-economy and showed his culinary skill off with pride to guests.

SALSA PANE E AGLIO
BREAD AND GARLIC SAUCE

◆

- 2 TBSP DRY BREADCRUMBS
- 2-3 CLOVES OF GARLIC
- 60 ML / 4 TBSP BROTH
- 1 TBSP VINEGAR
- PEPPER OR HOT RED PEPPER
- SALT
- OLIVE OIL

◆

PREPARATION TIME: 15 MINUTES

MOISTEN THE DRY BREADCRUMBS in the broth, season with salt and pepper (or hot red pepper), the chopped garlic, a trickle of olive oil and the vinegar. Stir well and serve. This sauce accompanies cold boiled meat.

VARIAION: for a stronger, more flavoursome sauce, toast the breadcrumbs slightly with two anchovy fillets in a little oil in a saucepan. Proceed to work the sauce as above.
It was precisely by means of these small additions and cooking procedures that the cook made an effort to impress the guests.

SALSA SARACENA
SARACENIC SAUCE

- 200 G / 8 OZ / 1⅓ CUPS PITTED (STONED) GREEN OLIVES
- 3 ANCHOVY FILLETS
- 25 G / 1 OZ / 3 TBSP WHITE FLOUR
- 20 G / ¾ OZ / 2 TBSP SULTANAS OR RAISINS
- 20 G / ¾ OZ / 3 TBSP PINE-NUTS
- 1 SACHET OF POWDERED SAFFRON
- PINCH OREGANO

PREPARATION TIME: 15 MINUTES

DISSOLVE THE ANCHOVY in a little oil in a saucepan (or rather an earthenware pot), add the olives, capers, sultanas and pine-nuts, all chopped up together. Mix the flour and saffron to a smooth paste with half a glass of hot water in a cup, pour into the pan, stir well and leave to blend for 5-10 minutes.

This sauce is excellent with boiled beef or chicken.

SALSA SFIZIOSA
SAUCE CAPRICE

- SPRIG OF PARSLEY
- 1 CELERY HEART
- 1 SMALL ONION
- 2 ANCHOVY FILLETS
- 2 PICKLED GHERKINS
- 30 G / 1 OZ / 2 TBSP PICKLED CAPERS
- GRATED ZEST AND JUICE OF 1 LEMON
- GRATED ZEST OF 1 ORANGE
- SALT AND PEPPER

PREPARATION TIME: 20 MINUTES

CHOP THE HERBS with the anchovies, gherkins, capers and the grated lemon and orange zest .

Mix well, alternating olive oil and lemon juice until you have obtained a thick, smooth sauce. Season with salt and pepper and serve with boiled fish.

SALSA VERDE

GREEN SAUCE

◆

- 30 G / 1 OZ / 2 TBSP CAPERS
- 3 ANCHOVY FILLETS
- 2-3 BASIL LEAVES
- ¼ ONION OR 1 SPRING ONION (SCALLION)
- 1 LEMON
- 1 HARD-BOILED EGG YOLK
- HANDFUL CHOPPED PARSLEY
- OLIVE OIL

◆

PREPARATION TIME: 20 MINUTES

CHOP UP THE CAPERS, anchovy, onion, basil, parsley and egg yolk in the food chopper. Add the olive oil, alternated with the lemon juice, continuing to blend until the sauce is nice and smooth.

This is excellent served with boiled meat. I advise you to get the sauce ready a few hours beforehand.

MEAT

"Carni e pisci, la vita ti crisci"
(Your life-span increases if you eat meat and fish)

E. Alaimo "Proverbi Siciliani" Edit. Martello

Meat-based second courses were for feast days, for growing children and for convalescents who had to regain their physical strength. There was not a great number of such dishes and the meat was proverbially tough, because the animals were exploited to the utmost for work in the fields before being sent to the slaughterhouse. Besides, the pasturage consisted of dry grass for many months in the year. The dishes most commonly found throughout Sicily were, accordingly, based on minced meat: meat balls, meat rolls, forcemeat.

On special occasions, calves were butchered so that dishes such as "falsomagro", "agglassatu", etc. could be prepared....

In certain periods of the year, lambs, chicken, pigs, rabbits and game were used in tasty dishes. Lamb was consumed at Easter, pork at Christmas and game when the animals passed through the territory.

AGNELLO IN UMIDO
STEWED LAMB

◆

- 1 KG / 2 LBS LAMB, IN CHUNKS
- 1 KG / 2 LBS POTATOES
- 100 G / 4 OZ PRIMOSALE OR ANOTHER FRESH, SAVOURY CHEESE
- 50 G / 2 OZ / 8 TBSP GRATED CHEESE (PECORINO OR PARMESAN)
- 2 CLOVES OF GARLIC
- 1 ONION
- 125 ML / 4 FL OZ / ½ CUP RED WINE
- SPRIG OF PARSLEY
- SALT
- PEPPER
- OIL

◆

PREPARATION TIME: 2 HOURS

TAKE A FRYING PAN (or preferably an earthenware pot) and sauté the chopped onion in a little oil, adding the garlic and parsley chopped up together and the chunks of meat. Turn to brown all over, pour on the red wine and cover with the lid.

Peel and cut up the potatoes, add to the lamb, season with salt and pepper and replace the lid. Continue cooking over gentle heat for about an hour.

Before serving, flavour with the sliced primosale and dredge with the grated cheese.

Some of the sauce may be used with pasta.

ARROSTO DI MAIALE AL LIMONE

LEMON-FLAVOURED PORK

- 800 G / 1¾ LBS LOIN OF PORK
- 3 LEMONS
- 1 KG / 2 LBS POTATOES (NEW ONES IF IN SEASON)
- 5 TBSP VEGETABLE OIL
- 10 WHITE PEPPERCORNS
- 1 CLOVE OF GARLIC
- ROSEMARY
- BAY LEAF
- WHITE FLOUR
- SALT

PREPARATION TIME: 1½ HOURS

COAT THE LOIN OF PORK in flour and sear in the oil in a meat tin (baking pan) with all the herbs and garlic. Add the peeled, finely-sliced potatoes and season with salt and pepper. Add the juice of three lemons, the grated zest of one lemon and a glass of water.
Roast in a hot oven for about an hour.

BOLLITO DI CARNE
BOILED MEAT

◆

- 1 KG / 2 LBS BRISKET OF BEEF
- 2 TOMATOES
- 2 ONIONS
- 2 POTATOES
- 1 MARROW BONE
- BAY LEAF
- A FEW PEPPERCORNS
- 1 STICK OF CELERY
- BUNCH OF PARSLEY
- SALT

◆

PREPARATION TIME: 3-4 HOURS

PUT COLD WATER to cover the meat in a saucepan, along with the parsley, celery, peppercorns, bay leaf and the tomatoes, skinned, seeded and roughly chopped. As soon as the water begins to boil, skim the surface and add the onions whole. Continue to cook for about 2 hours. Add the potatoes and cook a further hour over moderate heat.

MINT SAUCE is the classical accompaniment to boiled meat and is prepared many hours before it is needed. This is how to make it: emulsify some olive oil and vinegar, season with salt and pepper and pour the liquid onto the mint leaves. Mix well and leave to rest for as long as possible.

Here are the ingredients:
2 TABLESPOONS OLIVE OIL
SALT
PEPPER
A HANDFUL OF MINT LEAVES
60 ML / 2 FL OZ / ¼ CUP VINEGAR

91

CAPRETTO CON STRACCIATELLA
KID WITH EGG AND CHEESE BROTH

◆

- 1 KG / 2 LBS KID
- 5 EGGS
- 2 ONIONS
- 100 G / 4 OZ / 1 CUP GRATED PECORINO OR PARMESAN CHEESE
- SPRIG OF PARSLEY, CHOPPED
- SALT AND PEPPER
- OIL

◆

PREPARATION TIME: 2 HOURS

I N A RATHER LARGE SAUCEPAN (preferably an earthenware pot), brown the chopped onion in a little oil. Add the pieces of meat and, when golden, season with salt, pepper and chopped parsley. Cover with hot water and continue to cook over a slow flame for about an hour. Meanwhile, with a fork, beat the eggs in a bowl, together with the grated cheese, salt and pepper. Pour onto the kid and stir. If the gravy is too dry, add a little hot water. Keep over the heat for another 5 minutes before drawing it off.

The gravy can also be used as a sauce for pasta.

THIS EASTER DISH is found in the eastern area of Sicily. It is a dish for well-to-do families because the portions of kid do not have much meat in them. One kilogram of kid is enough for six people. The side-plate is usually a fry-up of mixed vegetables.

CONIGLIO ALL'AGRODOLCE
SWEET AND SOUR RABBIT

- 1 RABBIT, JOINTED
- 200 G / 8 OZ / 1⅓ CUPS PITTED (STONED) GREEN OLIVES
- 100 G / 4 OZ / ⅔ CUP WHITE FLOUR
- 50 G / 2 OZ / ¼ CUP CAPERS
- 25 G / 1 OZ / 2 TBSP GRANULATED SUGAR
- 1 ONION
- 1 STICK OF CELERY
- 125 ML / 4 FL OZ / ½ CUP OF VINEGAR
- 125 ML / 4 FL OZ / ½ CUP WHITE WINE

PREPARATION TIME: 1 HOUR

COAT THE RABBIT JOINTS in flour and fry in hot oil in a frying pan. Douse with the vinegar and sugar.

After a few minutes, once the liquid has evaporated, turn off the heat and cover the pan. Meanwhile, in a saucepan with a little oil, gently sauté the chopped onion, the celery cut into chunks, the pitted, roughly-chopped olives and the capers. Season with salt and pepper and, when it has all amalgamated, add the browned rabbit and cook for a further 20 minutes, sprinkling some white wine over if the sauce tends to dry up.

For a smoother sauce, chop up the onion, celery, olives and capers in an electric blender. The second stage of cooking may also be carried out in a hot oven.

93

COSCIOTTO DI AGNELLO RIPIENO

STUFFED LEG OF LAMB

◆

- 1 KG / 2 LBS BONED LEG OF LAMB
- 1 LAMB'S LIVER OR 300 G ¾ LB MINCED (GROUND) MEAT
- 500 G / 1 LB PEAS
- 4 SMALL ONIONS
- 1 MEDIUM-SIZED ONION, CHOPPED
- 150 G / 6 OZ BACON
- 50 G / 2 OZ / ½ CUP GRATED CACIOCAVALLO CHEESE
- 50 G / 2 OZ / ½ CUP DRY BREADCRUMBS
- 2 EGGS
- 125 ML / 4 FL OZ / ½ CUP WHITE WINE
- PARSLEY
- SALT AND PEPPER
- OIL

◆

PREPARATION TIME: 1½ HOURS

SAUTÉ TWO CHOPPED ONIONS in some oil in a saucepan. Add the peas, cover with water, season with salt and pepper and leave to cook over a low flame. In another saucepan, brown the two other onions which have been chopped up with the bacon, and the liver cut into pieces or the minced meat. Add a little water, season with salt and pepper and cook for 15-20 minutes until the sauce has reduced. Leave to cool, add the breadcrumbs, grated cheese, chopped parsley, peas and the beaten eggs. Blend the mixture evenly. Stuff the leg of lamb with it and tie or sew it up so that there is no spillage. Colour the chopped onion in a frying pan, add the stuffed leg and sear it. Pour in a glass of white wine and allow to evaporate. Season with salt and pepper and cover with the lid. Cook for another 45 minutes, adding hot water from time to time. Serve the leg hot, accompanied by the gravy in the pan.

FALSOMAGRO

STUFFED MEAT ROLL

◆

- 500 G / 1 LB SLICE OF BEEF (IN ONE PIECE)
- 300 G / ¾ LB MINCED (GROUND) BEEF
- 50 G / 2 OZ / ½ CUP DRY BREADCRUMBS
- 50 G / 2 OZ / 8 TBSP GRATED CHEESE (PECORINO OR PARMESAN)
- 3 EGGS, 2 OF THEM HARD-BOILED
- 125 ML / 4 FL OZ / ½ CUP DRY WHITE WINE
- 1 ONION
- 60 ML / 2 FL OZ / ¼ CUP MILK
- BASIL
- PARSLEY

◆

PREPARATION TIME: 3 HOURS

MIX THE MINCED MEAT with the cheese, breadcrumbs, milk, an egg, the chopped parsley, salt and pepper. Spread the mixture over the slice of beef, place the hard-boiled eggs lengthways, roll up the meat and tie it. In a saucepan, sauté the sliced onion in oil, add the "falsomagro" and allow to brown. Douse with wine and, when it has evaporated, cover the meat with hot water.

Cook gently until a thick gravy has formed (this makes an excellent sauce for serving with spaghetti).

———

VARIATION: you can cook the "falsomagro" in a moderate oven for about an hour; when half-cooked, add peeled potatoes in small chunks.

You can cook the meat in home-made tomato sauce and, should you wish to make it richer, add, half-way through, potatoes cut into chunks and/or peas.

You may use a different stuffing: replace the minced meat with an omelette (plain or with onions or aromatic herbs) and a slice of mortadella, all rolled up inside the meat slice.

Another kind of filling could be hard-boiled eggs, finely-sliced spring onions and fresh cheese (primosale or provola or caciocavallo or Tuscan or Sardinian caciottina, etc.).

GIRELLO ALLA PALERMITANA
VEAL PALERMO-STYLE

◆
- 1 KG / 2 LBS TOP ROUND OF VEAL
- 500 G / 1 LB WHITE-SKINNED ONIONS
- ¼ L / ½ PT / 1 CUP DRY WHITE WINE
- 250 ML / 8 FL OZ / 1 CUP OLIVE OIL
- 1 TBSP TOMATO CONCENTRATE
- BAY LEAF
- ROSEMARY
- SALT AND PEPPER
◆

PREPARATION TIME: 2 HOURS

SLICE THE ONIONS very finely and colour in half the olive oil over very low heat until well-cooked.

Sear the meat with the herbs and the remaining oil in a meat tin (baking pan). Add the cooked onions to the meat and pour on the wine. Season with salt and pepper.

Cook in a hot oven for about 90 minutes.

When the meat is ready, purée the onion gravy in a "mouli légumes" (food mill) and add the tomato concentrate to it.

Carve the meat thinly and serve masked in the onion sauce.

You could serve some of the cream of onions on macaroni noodles or spaghetti.

GIRELLO IMBOTTITO
STUFFED TOP ROUND OF VEAL

◆

- 800 G / 1¾ LBS TOP ROUND OF VEAL
- 50 G / 2 OZ SAVOURY PECORINO CHEESE
- 4 SLICES SALAMI, IN PIECES
- 2 CLOVES OF GARLIC, CHOPPED
- 1 ONION
- 2 TBSP TOMATO CONCENTRATE
- 125 ML / 4 FL OZ / 8 TBSP RED WINE
- 6 TBSP OIL
- MEAT STOCK
- SALT AND PEPPER

◆

PREPARATION TIME: 2 HOURS

MAKE A FEW SLITS in the piece of meat and fill up with cheese, garlic and salami. Season with salt and pepper. Tie the meat up well to keep the filling in. Sear the meat in a saucepan with the finely-sliced onion, turning frequently until brown all over.

Dissolve the tomato concentrate in the glass of red wine and douse the meat with it. When the wine has evaporated, add the meat stock a little at a time and cook over moderate heat for about an hour. Beware of the meat sticking to the pan.

POLPETTE AL SUGO
CROQUETTES WITH TOMATO SAUCE

- 500 G / 1 LB MINCED (GROUND) MEAT
- 1 KG / 2 LBS TOMATOES
- 80 G / 3 OZ / 12 TBSP GRATED CHEESE
- 50 G / 2 OZ / ½ CUP DRY BREADCRUMBS
- 50 G / 2 OZ CHOPPED MORTADELLA OR SKINLESS SAUSAGE
- 1 EGG
- 1 ONION
- 60 ML / 2 FL OZ / ¼ CUP MILK
- CHOPPED BASIL
- CHOPPED PARSLEY
- SALT AND PEPPER
- OIL

PREPARATION TIME: 45 MINUTES

MAKE THE SAUCE with the roughly-chopped tomatoes, the onion, basil and salt. Cook for 30 minutes and put through a vegetable mill. Meanwhile, in a bowl, mix the minced meat with the mortadella or sausage, the breadcrumbs, the grated cheese, the egg, salt and pepper, and aromatise with parsley and basil. Blend and, if necessary, add a little milk to make the mixture soft. Form little balls, which you will brown in some hot oil in a frying pan.

Transfer to the sauce and cook for 10 minutes.

VARIATION: "polpette" are the basis of Sicilian cuisine; each family has a secret recipe for making them. To the mixture described above, you may add garlic, onion, etc.… They may also be cooked in the sauce without browning them in oil beforehand. In this way, they are easier on the digestion.

POLPETTE ALL'AGRODOLCE

PATTIES IN A SWEET AND SOUR SAUCE

◆

- 700 G / 1½ LB MINCED (GROUND) VEAL
- 2 ONIONS
- 2 EGGS
- 100 G / 4 OZ / 1 CUP GRATED PARMESAN CHEESE
- 3 TBSP DRY BREADCRUMBS
- 30 ML / 4 TBSP MILK
- BUNCH OF PARSLEY
- 1 CLOVE OF GARLIC
- 1 BAY LEAF
- 100 G / 4 OZ / 1 CUP ALMONDS, PEELED AND TOASTED
- 60 ML / 2 FL OZ / ¼ CUP WHITE VINEGAR
- 2 TBSP SUGAR
- WHITE FLOUR
- SALT AND PEPPER
- HOT RED PEPPER (OPTIONAL)
- OIL

◆

PREPARATION TIME: 45 MINUTES

IN A BOWL, mix the minced meat with the eggs, the breadcrumbs softened in the milk, the grated Parmesan, the chopped garlic and parsley, salt and pepper. Blend the mixture thoroughly. Roll into little balls, flour and fry them. Prepare the sweet and sour sauce by cooking the sliced onions with oil, salt and hot red pepper for 10 minutes. Then add the vinegar, sugar and bay leaf. Continue cooking until the vinegar has completely evaporated.

Put the little drained balls into a large salad bowl, douse with the sweet and sour sauce straight off the heat and scatter the chopped almonds over.

This dish should be served just warm at room temperature.

POLPETTINE
MEAT BALLS

- 500 G / 1 LB MINCED (GROUND) MEAT
- 500 G / 1 LB ONIONS
- 100 G / 4 OZ / 1⅔ CUPS WHITE FLOUR
- 80 G / 3 OZ / 12 TBSP GRATED PECORINO OR PARMESAN CHEESE
- 50 G / 2 OZ / ½ CUP DRY BREADCRUMBS
- 1 EGG
- 1 BOILED POTATO
- SPRIG OF PARSLEY
- 60 ML / 2 FL OZ / ¼ CUP MILK
- BASIL
- SALT, PEPPER, AND OIL

PREPARATION TIME: 1 HOUR

PUT THE MEAT, grated cheese, bread, potato (mashed in a ricer) and the egg in a bowl. Season with salt and pepper and aromatise with the basil and parsley. Work the mixture together thoroughly, if necessary adding a little milk to soften it. Form tiny, round balls, which you will place on a large plate with the flour. Sweat the chopped or finely-sliced onion in a little oil in a pan, allowing it to colour without frying. Arrange the floured meat balls on the onion, stir carefully and cover with hot water. Check the salt and pepper and turn off the heat when the sauce is rather dense (excellent for serving on spaghetti).

THIS DISH used to be prepared on special occasions or for convalescents as it was considered easily digestible and very nutritious.

POLPETTONE
MEAT ROLL

- 700 G / 1½ LBS MINCED (GROUND) MEAT
- 200 G / 8 OZ FRESH SAUSAGE MEAT
- 200 G / 8 OZ PRIMOSALE CHEESE
- 100 G / 4 OZ VEGETABLES IN SEASON (GLOBE ARTICHOKES, COURGETTES/ZUCCHINI, SWISS CHARD OR SPINACH)
- 4 WHOLE EGGS
- 3 TBSP GRATED CACIOCAVALLO OR PECORINO OR PARMESAN OR ANOTHER RIPE CHEESE
- 3 TBSP DRY BREADCRUMBS
- 50 G / 2OZ SALAMI
- 125 ML / 4 FL OZ / ½ CUP DRY, WHITE WINE
- BUNCH OF PARSLEY
- 1 CLOVE OF GARLIC
- 30 ML / 2 TBSP MILK
- TWIG OF ROSEMARY
- SALT AND PEPPER
- OIL

PREPARATION TIME: 1½ HOURS

BOIL TWO EGGS until hard and the vegetables, separately. Mix the minced meat with two whole eggs, caciocavallo, breadcrumbs, milk and the chopped parsley and garlic in a bowl. Season with salt and pepper.

Work the mixture at length and, if it is too soft, add some grated cheese. Sprinkle a sheet of greaseproof (wax) paper with flour, spread the meat mixture out to form a rectangle and place the cooked vegetables, the sliced salami and hard-boiled eggs, the crumbled, uncooked sausage meat and the sliced primosale in the centre.

Make a meat roll by wrapping the greaseproof paper round, flour it and lay in a heated, oiled baking tin. Place the twig of rosemary on top.

Bake in a hot oven for 10 minutes. Turn it over, douse with a glass of white wine and continue cooking for another 45 minutes, sprinkling with more wine, if necessary.

POLLO ALL'ARANCIA
ORANGE-FLAVOURED CHICKEN

- 1 WHOLE CHICKEN
- 2 TBSP ORANGE MARMALADE
- JUICE OF 5 ORANGES
- BAY LEAF
- ROSEMARY
- SALT AND PEPPER

PREPARATION TIME: 1 HOUR

CLEAN THE CHICKEN WELL, dry it and spread the orange marmalade all round the body cavity. Brown in oil, along with the bay leaf and the rosemary.

When nicely coloured, pour in the orange juice to cover. Season with salt and pepper. Roast in a hot oven for an hour. Serve garnished with slices of orange.

POLLO AL VINO ROSSO
CHICKEN IN RED WINE

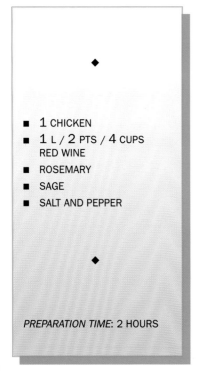

- 1 CHICKEN
- 1 L / 2 PTS / 4 CUPS RED WINE
- ROSEMARY
- SAGE
- SALT AND PEPPER

PREPARATION TIME: 2 HOURS

JOINT THE CHICKEN, rinse and dry it well. Arrange the chicken pieces in an oiled casserole. Season with the herbs, salt and pepper. Douse with red wine and bake in a moderate oven for about an hour.

VARIATION: you may add a handful of dried mushrooms, refreshed in hot water, or else 200 g (8 oz / 2 cups) fresh mushrooms.

102

POLLO RIPIENO
STUFFED CHICKEN

- 1 BONED CHICKEN
- 300 G / ¾ LB MINCED (GROUND) BEEF
- 150 G / 6 OZ CHICKEN LIVERS
- 100 G / 4 OZ / 1 CUP GRATED PECORINO OR PARMESAN CHEESE
- 50 G / 2 OZ / ½ CUP DRY BREADCRUMBS
- 2 EGGS
- 125-250 ML / ½ TO 1 CUP WHITE WINE
- BASIL
- PARSLEY
- SALT AND PEPPER
- OIL

PREPARATION TIME: 45 MINUTES

CHOP UP THE LIVERS AND SAUTÉ. In a bowl, place the minced beef, eggs, cheese, breadcrumbs, livers and the chopped basil and parsley. Season with salt and pepper, mix well and use to stuff the body cavity of the chicken. Sew up the opening so that the stuffing does not spill out.

Sear the chicken all over in oil in a meat tin (baking pan), pour on the wine and allow to evaporate. Transfer the tin to a moderate oven for 1½ hours.
Pour on some wine and hot water from time to time to keep the meat tender. Serve with roast potatoes.

VARIATION: the stuffed chicken may be cooked in stock: cover with water and throw in some parsley stalks, onion, a potato and a stick of celery. In this case, the accompaniments will be the same as for boiled meats.

SALSICCIA AL FORNO CON PATATE

BAKED SAUSAGES AND POTATOES

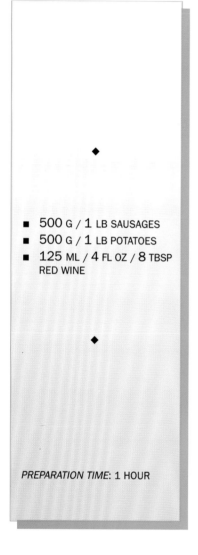

- 500 G / 1 LB SAUSAGES
- 500 G / 1 LB POTATOES
- 125 ML / 4 FL OZ / 8 TBSP RED WINE

PREPARATION TIME: 1 HOUR

PRICK OVER THE SAUSAGES so that they do not burst. Put into a roasting tin or dish with a little oil or just with the wine. Cook on the top of the stove until a froth of fat forms. Skim it off with a spoon, pour on some more wine and pop into a moderate oven for 10 minutes.

Turn the sausages over and add the potatoes cut into pieces. Continue cooking for a further 15-20 minutes.

SALSICCIA CON OLIVE NERE

SAUSAGES WITH BLACK OLIVES

◆

- 500 G / 1 LB SAUSAGES
- 200 G / 8 OZ / 1⅓ CUPS OLIVES
- 60 ML / 2 FL OZ / ¼ CUP WHITE WINE
- OIL

◆

PREPARATION TIME: 30 MINUTES

FRY THE SAUSAGES (pricked over with a fork) in a little oil in a frying pan. Toss in the olives and stir so that they absorb the frying oil. Drench with wine, allow to evaporate and turn off the heat. These marry well with boiled cauliflower, dressed with lemon and olive oil.

If you wish to remove the fat from the sausages, boil them in a little hot water before frying them. Then skim and fry.

SCALOPPE AL MARSALA
CUTLETS WITH MARSALA

- ◆ -

- 5-6 VEAL CUTLETS
- 125 ML / 4 FL OZ / ½ CUP DRY MARSALA
- WHITE FLOUR
- SALT AND PEPPER
- OIL

- ◆ -

PREPARATION TIME: 30 MINUTES

FLOUR THE CUTLETS and cook in a frying pan with a little oil. Turn them over and pour in the Marsala. Continue cooking until almost all the wine has evaporated and there is a thick gravy.

This is a speedily-prepared dish which resolves the dilemma of unexpected visitors.

Thin slices of chicken or turkey may also be used.

SPEZZATINO CON PATATE

STEW WITH POTATOES

- 1 KG / 2 LBS BEEF OR VEAL STEWING STEAK
- 500 G / 1 LB POTATOES
- 4-5 BASIL LEAVES
- 1 ONION
- 1 CLOVE OF GARLIC
- 125 ML / 4 FL OZ / ½ CUP WHITE WINE
- 1 TBSP HOME-MADE TOMATO SAUCE OR CONCENTRATE (OPTIONAL)
- SALT
- PEPPER

PREPARATION TIME: 1 HOUR

BROWN THE CHOPPED ONION and the whole garlic clove (to be removed once coloured) in some oil in a saucepan. Add the meat and allow the flavours to blend. Pour in the wine and let it evaporate for 5 minutes. Add the potatoes cut into small pieces and cover with hot water. Dress with the basil and tomato (if wished) and season with salt and pepper. Cook over a moderate flame for 30-40 minutes. Add water if necessary.

The sauce is excellent for serving over spaghetti.

VARIATION: Try replacing the potatoes with peas, or with globe artichokes to which you will add a little chopped parsley.

SPIEDINI

SPIT ROAST

♦

- 300 G / ¾ LB MINCED (GROUND) MEAT
- 250 G / ½ LB PRIMOSALE OR MILD PROVOLA
- 250 G / ½ LB SAUSAGES
- 100 G / 4 OZ / 1 CUP DRY BREADCRUMBS
- 50 G / 2 OZ / 8 TBSP GRATED PECORINO OR PARMESAN CHEESE
- 4 SLICES STALE BREAD
- 3 EGGS
- 1 SPRING ONION (SCALLION)
- 60 ML / 2 FL OZ / ¼ CUP MILK
- 60 ML / 2 FL OZ / ¼ CUP RED WINE
- BASIL LEAVES
- SALT AND PEPPER
- OIL FOR FRYING

♦

PREPARATION TIME: 1 HOUR

IN A BOWL, combine the minced meat with the grated cheese, half the breadcrumbs, an egg, the chopped onion, salt and pepper. Form little oval-shaped balls. Cook the sausages cut into little pieces in a little red wine in a frying pan. In the same pan, colour the bread soaked in the milk and cut into small cubes. Thread a piece of bread onto each skewer, followed by a meat ball, a dice of primosale cheese, a piece of sausage and finish up with some bread.

Beat the eggs and a pinch of salt in a bowl and turn the breadcrumbs onto a plate. Coat each skewer first in the egg, then in the breadcrumbs and fry in hot oil.

TRIPPA CON MELANZANE

TRIPE WITH AUBERGINE OR EGGPLANT

◆

- 1 KG / 2 LBS READY-COOKED TRIPE
- 500 G / 1 LB TINNED TOMATOES
- 3 AUBERGINES (EGGPLANTS)
- 4 TBSP GRATED PECORINO OR PARMESAN CHEESE
- 1 CLOVE OF GARLIC
- BASIL
- DRIED HOT RED PEPPER
- SALT
- OLIVE OIL

◆

PREPARATION TIME: 1½ HOURS

PREPARE THE TOMATO SAUCE with the tinned tomatoes and the garlic, hot red pepper, olive oil, salt and basil.

Arrange a layer of the tripe in a baking dish, then a layer of fried aubergine slices and cover with the sauce. Dredge with the grated cheese. Continue layering the ingredients until they have all been used up. Finish off with sauce and cheese. Bake in a hot oven for 30 minutes.

TRIPPA DI UOVA

OMELETTE IN TOMATO SAUCE

- 6 EGGS
- 500 G / 1 LB RIPE TOMATOES
- 100 G / 4 OZ / 1 CUP GRATED CHEESE
- 1 CLOVE OF GARLIC
- BASIL
- SALT AND PEPPER
- OLIVE OIL

PREPARATION TIME: 45 MINUTES

BEAT THE EGGS in a bowl, season with ⅔ of the grated cheese, salt and pepper. Pour half the eggs into a little oil in a frying pan and make an omelette. Remove from the pan and make a second one with the remaining eggs.

Cut the omelettes into strips. Meanwhile, sauté the whole garlic clove in a little oil in a pan, preferably an earthenware one. Add the skinned, seeded, roughly-chopped tomatoes, season with salt and pepper and add the chopped basil. Cook for 5 minutes, stirring well. Toss in the omelette strips and continue cooking for another 5 minutes. Arrange on a serving dish and dust with grated cheese.

FISH

"Carni metti carni,
pisci ti nutrisci.."
(Meat makes you stalwart, fish nurtures you)

F. Consolo *"La gastronomia nei proverbi"* Novedit Milano

Surrounded by three seas, Sicily has a great variety and quantity of fish ranging from bluefish to lobsters and shrimps of various sizes, right up to the swordfish, a sovereign fish.

There are humbler fish and more prized ones in sufficient quantity just to make sure that Sicilians do not suffer from hunger.

The recipes presented here are for fish which can be found fresh in most markets and also frozen nowadays. They are some time-honoured, tasty and nourishing recipes such as the "sarde a beccafico" or the tuna in a vinegar and onion sauce which used to be considered poor man's meals but which now find room on the menus of the best restaurants.

In the same way, the Benedictine nuns' "tortino di alici" used to be served as an appetiser in the baronial cuisine. I, however, have written it up as a main dish, because I find that it is complete when it follows a first course of pasta with seafood.

ALICI ALL'AGRODOLCE
FRESH ANCHOVIES IN A SWEET AND SOUR SAUCE

- 1 KG / 2 LBS FRESH ANCHOVIES, SCALED AND GUTTED
- 150 G / 6 OZ / 1 CUP WHITE FLOUR
- 60 ML / 2 FL OZ / ¼ CUP VINEGAR
- CLOVE OF GARLIC
- 25 G / 1 OZ / 2 TBSP GRANULATED SUGAR
- BAY LEAF
- FRESH MINT
- SALT AND PEPPER

PREPARATION TIME: 1 HOUR

COAT THE FISH with flour and fry. Sauté the garlic and bay leaf in a little oil in a pan. Add the vinegar with the sugar and cook for one or two minutes.

Draw off the heat and pour over the fried fish. Garnish with fresh mint.

VARIATION: fry the fish. In the same oil, put two crushed cloves of garlic with two or three tablespoons of water, a pinch of oregano and 4 tablespoons of vinegar. Boil for 10 minutes, then pour over the fish.

I recommend preparing this recipe a few days before serving it at the table.

ALICI DEL CONVENTO DELLE BENEDETTINE
GRATIN OF FRESH ANCHOVIES

◆

- 1 KG / 2 LBS FRESH ANCHOVIES, SCALED AND GUTTED
- 100 G / 4 OZ / ⅔ CUP GREEN OLIVES
- 50 G / 2 OZ / ½ CUP DRY BREADCRUMBS
- 30 G / 1 OZ / 1 TBSP PINE-NUTS
- 30 G / 1 OZ / 2 TBSP CAPERS
- 3 ORANGES
- 2 LEMONS
- BUNCH OF PARSLEY

◆

PREPARATION TIME: 1½ HOURS

ARRANGE THE SLICED, peeled lemon over the bottom of a baking dish and place the anchovies on top. Sprinkle with the olives, pine-nuts, parsley and capers, all chopped up together. Make another layer of lemons, anchovies and the chopped mixture. Top the final layer with the breadcrumbs, fried in a little oil. Bake in a hot oven for 30 minutes, add the orange juice and return to the oven for a further half-hour.

Allow me to make a valuable suggestion: when you peel the lemons, be careful to remove the white pith which would otherwise make the dish bitter.

ALICI IN POLPETTA
FRESH ANCHOVY FISHCAKES

♦

- 1 KG / 2 LBS FRESH ANCHOVIES OR SARDINES
- 3 MEDIUM-SIZED BOILED POTATOES
- 3 TBSP GRATED CACIOCAVALLO OR PARMESAN CHEESE
- 25 G / 1 OZ / 2½ TBSP RAISINS
- 25 G / 1 OZ / 2½ TBSP PINE-NUTS
- 2 LEMONS
- BUNCH OF PARSLEY
- 1 EGG
- 1 TBSP DRY BREADCRUMBS
- CLOVE OF GARLIC, CHOPPED
- FLOUR
- SALT AND PEPPER
- OIL FOR FRYING

♦

PREPARATION TIME: 1 HOUR

GUT AND SCALE THE FISH, rinse, drain well and chop up with a knife. Mix the fish with the egg, breadcrumbs, cheese, raisins and pine-nuts in a bowl. Add the chopped garlic and parsley and the mashed potatoes. Season with salt and pepper. Make small fishcakes, coat with flour and deep fry in oil. Serve hot with the lemon juice.

PICKLES were generally served with this dish (a mixture of vegetables: carrots, cauliflower, celery, etc., first blanched in water and vinegar and then preserved in oil or vinegar).

115

BACCALÀ AL FORNO
BAKED SALT COD

- 1 KG / 2 LB SALT COD, PREVIOUSLY SOAKED
- 500 G / 1 LB BOILED POTATOES
- 2 ONIONS
- 2 CLOVES OF GARLIC
- 3 CLOVES
- BUNCH OF PARSLEY,
- CHOPPED
- SALT AND PEPPER
- OLIVE OIL

PREPARATION TIME: 1½ HOURS

SLICE THE ONION FINELY. Boil the salt cod for 10 minutes, drain and leave to cool. Remove the skin and bones. Oil a baking tin or dish and arrange a layer of sliced potato in the bottom. Put half the salt cod fillets on top of the potatoes and scatter half the sliced onions over. Repeat the layers of potatoes, fish and onions. Season with pepper and the parsley, garlic and cloves, all chopped up. Sprinkle with oil and bake in a hot oven for an hour.

BACCALÀ IN INSALATA
SALT COD SALAD

- 1 KG / 2 LB SALT COD, PREVIOUSLY SOAKED
- 2 LEMONS
- SPRIG OF PARSLEY
- OLIVE OIL

PREPARATION TIME: 1 HOUR

RINSE THE SALT COD and place in a pan with the parsley and a few drops of vinegar. Cook for 15 minutes. Drain and allow to cool. Skin and bone the fish. Season with olive oil, lemon juice and chopped parsley.

VARIATION: chop up an onion and a clove of garlic and brown in a little oil in a pan. Add two or three ripe tomatoes cut into pieces. Cook for about 10 minutes and throw in 100 g (4 oz / ⅔ cup) pitted black olives.
Add the "baccalà", stir and scatter the chopped parsley over before drawing off the heat.

BACCALÀ IN SFINCIONE
SALT COD BAKED IN TOMATO SAUCE

- 1 KG / 2 LB SALT COD, PREVIOUSLY SOAKED
- 1 KG / 2 LB RIPE TOMATOES
- 200 G / 8 OZ / 1⅓ CUPS BLACK OLIVES, PITTED (STONED)
- 100 G / 4 OZ / 1 CUP DRY BREADCRUMBS
- 2 LARGE ONIONS
- SPRIG OF PARSLEY
- 60ML / 4 TBSP VINEGAR

PREPARATION TIME: 1½ HOURS

RINSE THE SALT COD and boil in water to which you have added a sprig of parsley and the vinegar. Drain and leave to cool. Skin and bone the fish and place in an oiled baking tin or ovenproof dish. Slice the onion finely and sauté in a pan with a little oil. Add the skinned, seeded and roughly-chopped tomatoes. Season with salt and pepper and cook for about 20 minutes until the sauce has thickened. Pour the sauce over the "baccalà", garnish with pieces of olive, sprinkle with breadcrumbs and oil and bake in a moderate oven for 20-30 minutes.

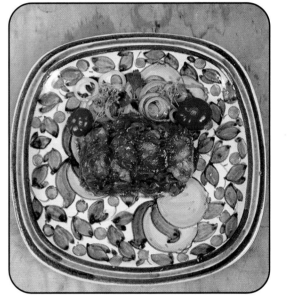

FILETTI DI ORATA CON CREMA DI ZUCCHINE
FILLETS OF GILTHEAD WITH COURGETTE PURÉE

- 12 FILLETS GILTHEAD OR SEA BREAM
- 24 BABY CLAMS
- 500 G / 1 LB COURGETTES (ZUCCHINI)
- 2 CLOVES OF GARLIC
- SPRIG OF PARSLEY
- 60 ML / 4 TBSP WHITE WINE
- 4 TBSP HOME-MADE TOMATO SAUCE
- WHITE FLOUR
- SALT AND PEPPER

PREPARATION TIME: 1 HOUR

CUT THE COUR-GETTES into rings and stew with oil, chopped parsley and garlic, salt, pepper and half a glass of water. As soon as it has all cooled, liquidise briefly. Meanwhile, clean the clams and put them in a pan over gentle heat until the shells open. Coat the fish fillets in flour and fry in a little oil.

Put the courgette purée into a wide baking tin or dish and arrange the gilthead or sea bream fillets and the clams on top. Moisten with the tomato sauce and the white wine and bake for 10 minutes in a hot oven.

117

PESCE SPADA A COTOLETTA
SWORDFISH CUTLETS

◆

- 4 SWORDFISH STEAKS (ABOUT 300 G / ½ LB EACH)
- 2 EGGS
- 2 LEMONS
- 100 G / 4 OZ / ⅔ CUP WHITE FLOUR
- 100 G / 4 OZ / 1 CUP DRY BREADCRUMBS
- CLOVE OF GARLIC
- PARSLEY
- SALT AND PEPPER

◆

PREPARATION TIME: 30 MINUTES

BEAT THE EGGS WITH A FORK. Take two plates; on one, mix the breadcrumbs with the chopped garlic and parsley, salt and pepper; on the other, put the flour. Heat some oil in a frying pan.

Dip each fish steak into the flour, then into the egg and finally coat with breadcrumbs. Fry in hot oil.

Arrange the cutlets on a serving dish and garnish with lemon wedges and parsley sprigs.

———————

THESE CUTLETS are generally served with boiled potatoes cut into small chunks and fried in really hot oil.

118

PESCE SPADA AL FORNO

BAKED SWORDFISH

- 4 SWORDFISH STEAKS
- 4 LEMONS
- 150 G / 6 OZ / 1½ CUPS DRY BREADCRUMBS
- 1 TSP OREGANO
- HOT RED PEPPER
- OLIVE OIL

PREPARATION TIME: 1½ HOURS

MACERATE THE FISH with the oil, lemon juice, grated zest of 1 lemon, oregano, salt and a pinch of hot red pepper for 30 minutes.

Dip the slices of fish into the breadcrumbs and arrange in an oiled oven dish. Bake for 30 minutes in a hot oven, remembering to turn the slices over half-way through.

Serve garnished with slices of lemon.

THIS IS A RICH MAN'S DISH because the fish must be very fresh and rather small.

Traditionally it is served with potatoes cooked over charcoal, but today jacket potatoes wrapped in aluminium foil and baked in the oven will do fine.

PESCE SPADA AL POMODORO
SWORDFISH IN TOMATO SAUCE

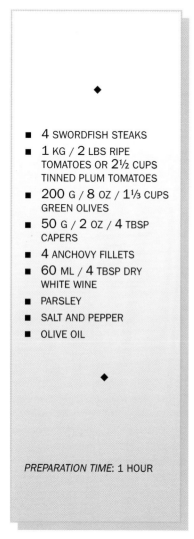

◆

- 4 SWORDFISH STEAKS
- 1 KG / 2 LBS RIPE TOMATOES OR 2½ CUPS TINNED PLUM TOMATOES
- 200 G / 8 OZ / 1⅓ CUPS GREEN OLIVES
- 50 G / 2 OZ / 4 TBSP CAPERS
- 4 ANCHOVY FILLETS
- 60 ML / 4 TBSP DRY WHITE WINE
- PARSLEY
- SALT AND PEPPER
- OLIVE OIL

◆

PREPARATION TIME: 1 HOUR

PUT INTO A PAN: the oil, the skinned, seeded and roughly-chopped tomatoes, the pitted olives cut into pieces, the capers and the anchovy fillets. Blend the flavours over a moderate heat for 5 minutes, add a glass of hot water and continue cooking for 20 minutes until the sauce becomes smooth. Arrange the slices of swordfish over the sauce, spray with white wine and cook a further 15-20 minutes.

Before drawing off the heat, dredge with salt, pepper and chopped parsley.

PESCE SPADA ALLA MESSINESE
SWORDFISH FROM MESSINA

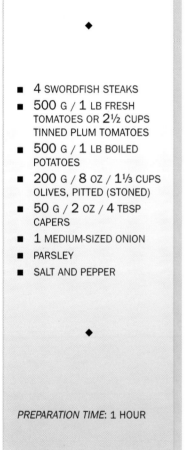

◆

- 4 SWORDFISH STEAKS
- 500 G / 1 LB FRESH TOMATOES OR 2½ CUPS TINNED PLUM TOMATOES
- 500 G / 1 LB BOILED POTATOES
- 200 G / 8 OZ / 1⅓ CUPS OLIVES, PITTED (STONED)
- 50 G / 2 OZ / 4 TBSP CAPERS
- 1 MEDIUM-SIZED ONION
- PARSLEY
- SALT AND PEPPER

◆

PREPARATION TIME: 1 HOUR

SAUTÉ THE CHOPPED ONION in a large pan. Add the roughly-chopped olives and tomatoes (skinned and seeded) and the capers. Cook slowly for 10 minutes. Arrange half of the sliced potatoes in a roomy, oiled baking dish, cover with the swordfish slices and mask with the sauce. Cover it all with the remaining potato. Bake in a moderate oven for about 20 minutes. Take the dish out of the oven, remove the top layer of potato and season the fish with salt, pepper and chopped parsley. Return to the switched-off oven which is still warm. Serve when a moderate temperature has been reached.

121

PESCE SPADA IN INVOLTINO
SWORDFISH ROLLS

◆

- **12** SWORDFISH STEAKS
- **150** G / **6** OZ / **1½** CUPS DRY BREADCRUMBS, FRIED IN OIL
- **6** FRESH ANCHOVY FILLETS IN OIL
- **2** CHOPPED CLOVES OF GARLIC
- **2** LEMONS
- **1** ONION
- A FEW BAY LEAVES
- SALT
- HOT RED PEPPER

◆

PREPARATION TIME: 1 HOUR

DISSOLVE THE FRESH ANCHOVY fillets in their oil over low heat. Add the breadcrumbs, the chopped garlic, the salt and hot red pepper. Spread the filling over the fish steaks and roll them up tightly. Thread them onto a skewer, alternating them with a piece of onion and a bay leaf. Sprinkle oil and lemon juice over. Bake in a moderate oven for 20 minutes, being careful that nothing dries out. The swordfish must be sliced thinly for this dish.

RUOTA DI PESCE SPADA AL FORNO
BAKED SWORDFISH WHEEL

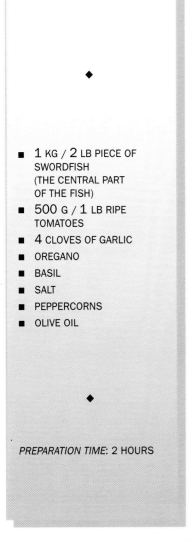

♦

- 1 KG / 2 LB PIECE OF SWORDFISH (THE CENTRAL PART OF THE FISH)
- 500 G / 1 LB RIPE TOMATOES
- 4 CLOVES OF GARLIC
- OREGANO
- BASIL
- SALT
- PEPPERCORNS
- OLIVE OIL

♦

PREPARATION TIME: 2 HOURS

QUARTER THE GARLIC CLOVES. Stud the fish with the garlic and the pepper corns. Cover the base of a baking dish with some of the tomatoes, skinned, seeded and roughly-chopped. Season with salt and arrange the fish on top. Cover with the remaining pieces of tomato, season with oregano, basil, salt and oil. Bake in a moderate oven for an hour and a half. Serve with potatoes grilled over charcoal or oven-baked in aluminium foil.

PESCE STOCCO ALLA GHIOTTA
SMOTHERED STOCKFISH

◆

- 1 KG / 2 LBS STOCKFISH, PREVIOUSLY SOAKED
- 4 SPRING ONIONS (SCALLIONS) OR SMALL ONIONS
- 100 G / 4 OZ / ½ CUP PICKLED CAPERS
- 100 G / 4 OZ / ⅔ CUP PITTED (STONED) BLACK OLIVES
- SMALL HEAD OF CELERY
- 500 G / 1 LB TIN (CAN) PLUM TOMATOES (2½ CUPS)
- 500 G / 1 LB POTATOES
- 125 ML / 8 TBSP DRY WHITE WINE
- WHITE FLOUR
- HOT RED PEPPER
- OIL

◆

PREPARATION TIME: 1½ HOUR

IN A DEEP FRYING PAN, sauté the spring onions cut into strips with the floured pieces of fish. Add the capers, the celery cut into rings, the potatoes in small chunks and the olives. Moisten with a glass of white wine which you will allow to evaporate. Add the tomatoes and cook slowly for about an hour.

If necessary, pour on a little water during the cooking, so that the sauce is not so thick.

POLIPETTI IN TEGAME
STEWED MOSCARDINI

- 1 KG / 2 LBS MOSCARDINI OR SQUID
- 400 G / 14 OZ / 2 CUPS TINNED TOMATOES
- 1 SMALL ONION
- CLOVE OF GARLIC
- BUNCH OF PARSLEY
- 60 ML / 2 FL OZ / ¼ CUP WHITE WINE
- WHITE FLOUR
- SALT
- HOT RED PEPPER

PREPARATION TIME: 1 HOUR

CLEAN THE "MOSCARDINI" and leave to drain. Coat with flour. Sauté the chopped onion and garlic in a pan. Add the "moscardini" and brown well, then douse with the white wine. When it has completely evaporated, add the skinned tomatoes. Continue cooking for 30 minutes over gentle heat.

Sprinkle with chopped parsley before drawing off the heat.

RONDELLE DI PALOMBO
PALOMBO IN TOMATO SAUCE

- 12 PALOMBO FISH FILLETS
- 2 CLOVES OF GARLIC
- 500 G / 1 LB / 2½ CUPS TINNED TOMATOES
- 3 EGGS
- SPRIG OF PARSLEY
- 1 KG / 2 LBS / 8 CUPS DRY BREADCRUMBS
- WHITE FLOUR
- SALT AND PEPPER
- HOT RED PEPPER

PREPARATION TIME: 30 MINUTES

RUB SOME SALT and pepper into the fish fillets, coat with flour and steep in the beaten egg for a few hours.

Meanwhile, chop up the garlic and parsley, add the tomatoes and cook the sauce for 15 minutes.

Add salt and hot red pepper. Dip the fish into the breadcrumbs and fry.

Add the fried fish fillets to the sauce and cook for 10 more minutes.

125

SARDE A BECCAFICO
STUFFED SARDINES

- 1 KG / 2 LBS FRESH SARDINES (IN AN EVEN NUMBER)
- 100 G / 4 OZ / 1 CUP DRY BREADCRUMBS
- 10 ALMONDS, TOASTED AND CHOPPED
- 10 BAY LEAVES
- 8 PITTED (STONED) BLACK OLIVES
- 6 ANCHOVY FILLETS, TINNED OR FRESH
- ZEST OF 2 LEMONS
- 2 TSP GRANULATED SUGAR
- HANDFUL OF PARSLEY
- 1 TBSP PICKLED CAPERS
- 1 TBSP EACH SULTANAS AND PINE-NUTS
- 60 ML / 4 TBSP LEMON JUICE

PREPARATION TIME: 1 HOUR

GUT THE SARDINES, pull off the head and backbone and open up flat. Rinse and dry. Dissolve the anchovies in heated oil, add the breadcrumbs and stir. When cold, add the grated lemon zest, 2 tablespoons sugared lemon juice, the chopped parsley, the capers, sultanas, pine-nuts, olives, almonds, salt and pepper. Stir and add a little olive oil if too dry. Spread the mixture over half the sardines, arrange in an oiled-and-crumbed baking dish and top with the remaining sardines.

Sprinkle with the rest of the lemon juice, place a bay leaf between each fish, trickle over a little olive oil and bake in a hot oven for 15 minutes.

THIS DISH gets its name from a bird very partial to figs which gets plumper and plumper the more it eats. Likewise, this fish "parcel" encourages the most uncontrolled voracity.

SEPPIE IN TEGAME
SMOTHERED CUTTLEFISH

◆

- 1 KG / 2 LBS CUTTLEFISH
- 50 G / 2 OZ / ¼ CUP TOMATO CONCENTRATE
- 1 ONION
- CLOVE OF GARLIC
- 125 ML / 8 TBSP WHITE WINE
- SPRIG OF PARSLEY

◆

PREPARATION TIME: 2 HOURS

GUT AND CLEAN the cuttlefish, removing the sacs of black ink, and cut into rings. Sauté the chopped onion and garlic in some oil in a pan. Add the cuttlefish, salt and pepper. Stir well and pour in the tomato concentrate diluted in the wine. Cook for 20 minutes over a moderate heat.

SGOMBRI ARROSTITI
GRILLED MACKEREL

- 4 MACKEREL
- 250 ML / 8 FL OZ / 1 CUP VINEGAR
- 2 LEMONS
- PINCH OF OREGANO
- SALT
- PEPPER

PREPARATION TIME: 1 HOUR

GUT, BONE AND CLEAN THE MACKEREL, opening them out flat. Marinate in a vinegar-filled bowl for 20 minutes. Drain and grill. Make the "salmoriglio" sauce to baste the fish by chopping up the oregano, salt and pepper with some oil and the lemon juice.

VARIATION: Clean the mackerel, leaving them whole. Make short slits along the body and insert pieces of garlic. Leave the mackerel to steep in a bowl with lemon juice, salt, garlic and chopped parsley and to absorb the flavours. Grill (Broil) them, brushing the marinade over with a sprig of rosemary.

127

SGOMBRI IN COTOLETTA
MACKEREL CUTLETS

- 6 MEDIUM-SIZED MACKEREL
- 3 EGGS
- 200 G / 8 OZ / 2 CUPS DRY BREADCRUMBS
- 1 TBSP GRANULATED SUGAR
- 125 ML / 8 TBSP WHITE WINE VINEGAR
- WHITE FLOUR
- SALT
- HOT RED PEPPER

PREPARATION TIME: 1 HOUR

GUT, BONE, CLEAN AND DRY THE MACKEREL, opening them out flat. Arrange in a bowl and cover with vinegar, salt and hot red pepper. Leave to marinate an hour. Drain the fish, coat with flour, then dip in the beaten egg and finally in the breadcrumbs. Deep fry in olive oil and serve hot.

THIS IS THE FISHERMAN'S Sunday dinner. Blue fish, tuna and sea food used to be poor man's meat. Cutlets were a noble dish and, together with a side-plate of fried potatoes, were a meal fit for a king. A scrumptious dish served after pasta in a seafood sauce.

TONNO CON LE CIPOLLE E L'ACETO
TUNA IN A VINEGAR AND ONION SAUCE

- 4 FRESH TUNA FISH SLICES
- 2-3 TOMATOES
- 2 ONIONS
- 100 G / 4 OZ / ⅔ CUP GREEN OLIVES
- 50 G / 2 OZ / ¼ CUP CAPERS
- 50 G / 2 OZ / ¼ CUP WHITE FLOUR
- 1 STICK OF CELERY
- 60 ML / 4 TBSP VINEGAR
- SALT AND PEPPER
- OLIVE OIL

PREPARATION TIME: 1 HOUR

COAT THE TUNA SLICES in flour and fry. Sauté the thinly-sliced onion in a little oil in a saucepan, add the chopped celery, the capers and the pitted olives cut into pieces. After 5 minutes, add the skinned, seeded and roughly-chopped tomatoes with a glass of hot water.
Cook until the sauce has reduced. Lay the tuna slices on top, spray with vinegar and, when it has evaporated, draw off the heat.

THIS RECIPE used to be prepared when the tuna catch was particularly copious.
The dish keeps for several days and is very good eaten cold. In this case, there must be plenty of "stemperata", the vinegar and onion sauce.

128

DESSERTS AND CONFECTIONERY

"Cosi amari, tènili cari
cosi duci, tènili 'nchiusi"
(Look after sour things carefully,
keep sweet things locked up)

E. Alaimo "Proverbi Siciliani" Edit. Martello

When you go into a Sicilian pastry shop, you are met with such a variety of fragrance, colour and choice of sweetmeats that deciding what to eat or buy is difficult. The basic ingredients of these desserts are honey, ricotta cheese, almonds, pistachios and lots of imagination.

They used to be made in the home as pastry shops were very few and many were attached to convents where the nuns made very refined sweet dishes to order.

When sweetmeats were made at home, the women started preparing them several weeks ahead of the religious or secular festivals and, while they worked, their grandmothers or elderly aunts (who directed and supervised the proceedings) would keep the children occupied by getting them to recite prayers or sing sacred hymns. So it is that the names of many sweet dishes are linked to the event or saint that was being celebrated. Two very distinct sweet dishes are associated with Easter: marzipan "sheep" and cassata. Even abroad, these have become the symbol of Sicilian desserts on account of the elegant way in which they are presented as well as for their delectability. It was the Arabs who, around 1200, taught the convent nuns the art of making marzipan and cassata. The story goes that, on the occasion of the Diocesan Synod at Mazara del Vallo, the nuns were forbidden to produce these sweets during Holy Week so as not to get distracted from their religious functions. Nowadays, the preparation is considered too complex and laborious, so very few people get round to making them at home. The cassata recipe that I give here is a simple one, without the marzipan decoration which requires skills of "haute cuisine".

Many recipes which belong to the tradition of Sicilian sweetmeats have been lost because they have not stood up to the recent competition of industrial pastry production which, in Sicily, too, has prevailed over home-cooking in the same domain.

BISCOTTI DI MANDORLE
ALMOND BISCUITS (COOKIES)

◆

- 500 G / 1 LB / 5 CUPS CHOPPED ALMONDS
- 500 G / 1 LB / 2½ CUPS GRANULATED SUGAR
- 6 EGG WHITES
- 1 EGG YOLK
- GRATED ZEST OF 1 LEMON
- 125 ML / 4 FL OZ / ½ CUP MILK
- PINCH CINNAMON
- PINCH SALT

◆

PREPARATION TIME: 30 MINUTES

TURN THE ALMONDS, sugar, grated lemon rind, cinnamon, milk and salt into a bowl and stir well. Whisk the egg whites until stiff and fold gently into the milk mixture. Spoon into a pastry bag. Pipe rounds onto a greased baking tray (or else line it with baking paper). Place an almond in the centre of each one and bake in a hot oven for ten minutes. Remove and brush the biscuits with beaten egg yolk. Return to the hot oven for another 10 minutes.

In my family, these biscuits used to be made at the beginning of December and then kept until Christmas.

131

BISCOTTI PEPATI
SPICY BISCUITS (COOKIES)

- 500 G / 1 LB / 3½ CUPS WHITE FLOUR
- 150 G / 6 OZ / ¾ CUP GRANULATED SUGAR
- 150 G / 6 OZ / 1½ CUPS CHOPPED ALMONDS
- 100 G / 4 OZ / ½ CUP HONEY
- 50 G / 2 OZ / 4 TBSP LARD OR BUTTER
- PINCH BICARBONATE OF SODA (BAKING SODA)
- PINCH NUTMEG
- PINCH CLOVES
- PINCH CINNAMON
- PINCH PEPPER

PREPARATION TIME: 30 MINUTES

WORK THE FLOUR, sugar and almonds with the butter, honey (dissolved in a little warm water), spices and bicarbonate. Roll into thick fingers which you will place on a greased baking try.
Bake in a hot oven for 10-15 minutes until the biscuits turn golden. Remove the tray from the oven, leave to cool a little, then cut the fingers into slices ½ in thick. Return to the oven for 5 minutes, then turn it off and leave the biscuits to cool inside before removing them.

BISCOTTI REGINA
SESAME BISCUITS (COOKIES)

- 300 G / ¾ LB / 2 CUPS WHITE FLOUR
- 200 G / 8 OZ / 1 CUP LARD OR BUTTER
- 100 G / 4 OZ / ½ CUP GRANULATED SUGAR
- 100 G / 4 OZ / 6 TBSP SESAME SEEDS
- 1 EGG
- PINCH SALT

PREPARATION TIME: 30 MINUTES (PLUS AN HOUR'S REST FOR THE DOUGH)

HEAP THE FLOUR, a pinch of salt and the sugar on a pastry board. Work in the egg and lard or soft butter (not melted). Knead gently until the flour is completely absorbed. If necessary, add half a glass of warm water.

Shape into a ball, wrap in a tea cloth and leave to rest in a warm place for about an hour.

Make fat fingers like breadsticks and cut into lengths of about 2-2½ in. Turn the sesame seeds into a bowl, roll the fingers in them and place on a greased baking try. Bake in a hot oven for about 20 minutes.

133

BISCOTTI TARALLE
ICED BISCUITS (COOKIES)

◆

- 500 G / 1 LB / 3½ CUPS WHITE FLOUR
- 500 G / 1 LB / 3½ CUPS CORNFLOUR (CORNSTARCH)
- 500 G / 1 LB / 2½ CUPS GRANULATED SUGAR
- 200 G / 8 OZ / 1⅔ CUPS ICING (CONFECTIONERS') SUGAR
- 6 EGGS
- 1 TBSP LARD OR BUTTER
- 1 SACHET / ¼ TSP VANILLA POWDER / ½ TSP VANILLA EXTRACT
- 60 ML / 4 TBSP MILK
- 60 ML / 4 TBSP PLAIN OR JASMINE-FLAVOURED WATER

◆

PREPARATION TIME: 40 MINUTES

SEPARATE THE EGG whites from the yolks. Beat the yolks and sugar to a smooth cream with the sugar. Sprinkle in the flour and cornflour and mix well, adding a little milk. Whisk the egg whites into stiff peaks and gently fold into the flour mixture until evenly blended. Either pipe the mixture from a piping bag or spoon it onto a greased baking tray to form fingers or rings and bake in a moderate oven for about 20 minutes.

To make the glacé icing (frosting), dissolve the icing sugar and the vanilla in the water and heat to just under boiling point. Before turning off the oven, brush the biscuits with the icing. Return to the still-warm oven and leave until it cools off.

BISCOTTI SPAGNOLETTE
RICOTTA BISCUITS (COOKIES)

◆

- 250 G / ½ LB / 1¼ CUPS GRANULATED SUGAR
- 250 G / ½ LB / 1¾ CUPS WHITE FLOUR
- GRATED ZEST OF 1 LEMON
- 25 G / 1 OZ / 2 TBSP VANILLA SUGAR
- 300 G / ¾ LB RICOTTA
- CHEESE
- 3 EGGS
- MILK

◆

PREPARATION TIME : 1 HOUR

CREAM THE YOLKS with 150 g (6 oz / ¾ cup) sugar. When you have a smooth foam, add the flour and the grated lemon zest a little at a time. Crush the ricotta in a bowl with 100 g (4 oz / ½ cup) sugar and work it in with a fork to get a smooth mixture. A little milk may be added to make it creamier. Whisk the egg whites until stiff and add the vanilla sugar. Slowly mix the ricotta into the creamed yolks and fold in the whisked egg whites. When the mixture is well blended, put some into a piping bag and pipe onto an oiled iron or aluminium baking tray in rounds. Repeat, using up all the paste, and bake for 20 minutes in a hot oven.

BUCCELLATO
DOUGH RING

- 300 G / ¾ LB / 2 CUPS WHITE FLOUR
- 150 G / 6 OZ / ¾ CUP LARD OR BUTTER
- 100 G / 4 OZ / ½ CUP GRANULATED SUGAR
- 125 ML / 4 FL OZ / 8 TBSP MARSALA
- 300 G / ¾ LB / 2 CUPS RAISINS
- 300 G / ¾ LB / 2 CUPS FIGS, CUT UP
- 100 G / 4 OZ / 1 CUP TOASTED ALMONDS
- 100 G / 4 OZ / ½ CUP PLAIN (SEMI-SWEET) CHOCOLATE, BROKEN UP
- 50 G / 2 OZ / ½ CUP WALNUTS, SHELLED
- 1 EGG YOLK
- 50 G / 2 OZ / ½ CUP CHOPPED PISTACHIOS
- PINCH OF CINNAMON
- PINCH OF SALT
- 1 LEMON

PREPARATION TIME: 3 HOURS

WORK THE LARD or butter into the sugar and flour on a pastry board, together with half the Marsala and a pinch of salt. When you have obtained a smooth dough, wrap in a tea towel and leave to rest for about two hours.

Prepare the filling by putting into a saucepan the cut-up figs, the toasted almonds (roughly chopped up with the walnuts), the grated lemon zest, the chocolate, the remaining Marsala and a pinch of cinnamon. Simmer over low heat for about 20 minutes, stirring frequently.

With the aid of a rolling pin, roll the dough into a rectangle about ½ in thick. Pour the cooled filling into the centre, roll up the dough and join the ends to make a ring. Pierce the surface with a fork and place on a greased baking tray. Bake in a hot oven for 30 minutes. Remove the tray from the oven.

Beat an egg yolk energetically and, using a pastry brush or a little cotton wool, spread it over the dough ring. Sprinkle with the chopped pistachios and bake a further 5 minutes. Turn off the oven and leave to cool before removing the cake.

CANNOLI
RICOTTA-FILLED SNAPS

◆

- 150 G / 6 OZ / 1 CUP WHITE FLOUR
- 15 G / ½ OZ / ½ TBSP BITTER COCOA
- 30 G / 1 OZ / 2 TBSP LARD OR BUTTER
- 1 EGG
- 25 G / 1 OZ / 2 TBSP GRANULATED SUGAR
- 60 ML / 2 FL OZ / ¼ CUP RED WINE OR MARSALA
- 12 STEEL TUBES
- OIL

THE FILLING:
- 500 G / 1 LB / 2¾ CUPS RICOTTA CHEESE
- 250 G / 8 OZ / 2 CUPS ICING (CONFECTIONERS') SUGAR
- 100 G / 4 OZ PLAIN (SEMI-SWEET) CHOCOLATE, DICED
- 80 G / 3 OZ / ⅜ CUP CANDIED PUMPKIN
- 50 G / 2 OZ PISTACHIOS, CHOPPED
- PINCH CINNAMON
- CANDIED ORANGE PEEL

◆

PREPARATION TIME: 4 HOURS

HEAP THE FLOUR on a pastry board and carefully work in the egg, lard or butter, sugar, the cocoa dissolved in the red wine or Marsala, and a pinch of salt. When you have a smooth dough, leave to rest for about an hour. With a rolling pin, roll it out into a thin sheet and cut into 4 inch squares. Roll each one diagonally around a steel tube. Delicately press the edges together with a dampened finger. Heat plenty of oil in a deep saucepan and, when it is boiling, immerse the dough-covered tubes. Remove the snaps when they have turned golden and allow to cool.

Meanwhile, work the ricotta with the icing sugar and the cinnamon. Mix well with a wooden spoon, adding a few drops of milk. The cream should be smooth and rather thick. Add the diced chocolate and candied pumpkin at this point, then carefully remove the tubes from the "cannoli" and fill them with a teaspoonful of the filling.

Garnish with pieces of candied orange peel which you will stick into the ends. Dredge the biscuit (cooky) part with a little icing sugar.

CARAMELLE DI CARRUBE

CAROB SQUARES

◆

- 200 G / 8 OZ / 1 CUP HONEY
- 200 G / 8 OZ CAROB PODS
- OIL

◆

PREPARATION TIME: 30 MINUTES

BREAK THE CAROB PODS TO EXTRACT THE SEEDS. Heat them very gently with the honey in a small saucepan. Stir from time to time and when the mixture has become syrupy and caramelised, pour onto an oiled marble slab. Spread the caramel out with a spatula to a thickness of ½ inch . Cut into little squares and leave to dry. They will keep in glass jars.

Even street vendors in Sicily used to sell these sweets. Grandmothers would give them to their grandchildren to suck, especially as a remedy against coughs.

A few decades ago, they disappeared off the market and, unfortunately also from the domestic kitchen.

CASSATA CASALINGA

SICILIAN CASSATA

◆

- 500 G / 1 LB
  SPONGE CAKE
- 500 G / 1 LB
  RICOTTA CHEESE
- 300 G / ¾ LB / 2 CUPS
  ICING (CONFECTIONERS')
  SUGAR
- 100 G / 4 OZ PLAIN
  (SEMI-SWEET) CHOCOLATE
- PINCH GROUND CINNAMON
- SACHET / ¼ TSP VANILLA
  POWDER OR ½ TSP EXTRACT
- 50 G / 2 OZ / ½ CUP
  PISTACHIOS
- 60 ML / 2 FL OZ / 4 TBSP
  VERMOUTH
- 50 G / 2 OZ / ¼ CUP
  CANDIED FRUIT

◆

PREPARATION TIME: 2 HOURS

CUT THE SPONGE CAKE into rectangular slices and place half of them side by side on the bottom of a springform baking tin (with removable sides).

Sprinkle with the vermouth. Work the icing sugar and a few drops of milk into the ricotta to get a creamy mixture, add the diced candied fruit and chocolate, the cinnamon, vanilla and pistachios.

Pour the cream onto the sponge slices, cover with another layer of cake, dust with icing sugar and garnish with the candied fruit.

Chill in the refrigerator for a few hours, but do not freeze.

138

CASSATINE DI CARNEVALE

CASSATA PASTRIES

◆

- 500 G / 1 LB / 3½ CUPS WHITE FLOUR
- 60 ML / 2 FL OZ / 4 TBSP OLIVE OIL
- PINCH OF SALT
- 500 G / 1 LB RICOTTA CHEESE
- 200 G / ½ LB / 1 CUP GRANULATED SUGAR
- 100 G / 4 OZ / ½ CUP PLAIN (SEMI-SWEET) CHOCOLATE
- PINCH GROUND CINNAMON

◆

PREPARATION TIME: 2 HOURS

KNEAD THE FLOUR WITH THE OIL, salt and a little warm water until the dough is even and elastic. Wrap in a tea towel and leave to rest for about an hour. Make the filling by working the sugar and cinnamon into the ricotta. When you have a creamy mixture, add the diced chocolate.

Roll out the pastry into a thin sheet with a rolling pin. Cut out rounds by pressing an upturned teacup down into the pastry. Put a spoonful of the cream in the centre of each one and close it over, lightly pinching the edges together with your dampened fingers.

Arrange the pastries on a greased baking tray and bake for 40 minutes in a moderate oven.

VARIATION: the pastries may be fried in hot oil or lard and dredged with icing (confectioners') sugar while still hot.

CREMA BIANCO MANGIARE

BLANCMANGE

◆

- 1 L / 2 PINTS / 4 CUPS MILK
- 100 G / 4 OZ / ½ CUP GRANULATED SUGAR
- 100 G / 4 OZ / ¾ CUP CORNFLOUR (CORNSTARCH)
- 1 LEMON

◆

PREPARATION TIME: 30 MINUTES

PUT THE SUGAR, corn-flour and grated lemon zest in a saucepan. Little by little, pour over the cold milk, stirring constantly so that lumps do not form. When everything is completely dissolved, place over the heat and continue stirring until the cream looks smooth and comes away easily from the sides of the pan. Draw off the heat. Pour into bowls and leave to cool.

———————————————

VARIATIONS: you can replace the grated lemon zest with 2 teaspoons of bitter cocoa, or with an egg yolk, or with a pinch of vanilla. You may enrich it with finger biscuits, onto which you pour the cream with your chosen flavour. Children love it.

CREMA DI ANGURIA

WATER MELON CUSTARD

◆

- 1 WATERMELON, ABOUT 5 KG / 11 LB
- 100 G / 4 OZ / ½ CUP GRANULATED SUGAR EVERY LITRE (2 PT / 5 CUPS) MELON JUICE
- 80 G / 3 OZ / ½ CUP CORNFLOUR (CORN STARCH) EVERY LITRE (2 PT / 5 CUPS) MELON JUICE
- 80 G / 3 OZ / ⅜ CUP CANDIED PUMPKIN SHREDS
- 100 G / 4 OZ / ½ CUP PLAIN (SEMI-SWEET) CHOCOLATE
- JASMINE WATER FROM THE FLOWERS (OPTIONAL)

◆

PREPARATION TIME: 3 HOURS

STEEP THE JASMINE PETALS IN WATER AND FILTER. Slice the watermelon, discard the seeds and the peel and sieve the pulp. Pour the resultant juice into a saucepan, add the sugar, the cornflour dissolved in the melon juice, and the jasmine flower water.

Heat the saucepan and cook the liquid, stirring constantly until it has thickened. Draw off from the heat and pour the custard into bowls and leave to cool. Cut the candied pumpkin and the plain chocolate to pieces and distribute between the bowls.

This is a very fragrant summer sweet. In Palermo, they make pies of short pastry filled with this "gelu di miluni".

———————————————

CANDIED PUMPKIN or zuccata is exclusively Sicilian. It is sold in fine, ribbon-like shreds.

CREMA DI MANDARINI
TANGERINE CUSTARD

- **10** TANGERINES
- **100** G / 4 OZ / ¾ CUP CORNFLOUR (CORNSTARCH)
- **100** G / 4 OZ / ½ CUP GRANULATED SUGAR

PREPARATION TIME: 3-4 HOURS

CAREFULLY REMOVE THE "LID" from each tangerine. Pull out the segments, leaving the peel intact. Collect the juice from the segments which you will squeeze into a saucepan to obtain 1 litre (2 pints / 4 cups) of juice. Gradually add the sugar and the cornflour. Heat, stirring well, until the cream is thick.

Remove from the top of the stove and pour into the tangerine skins. Cover with the "lids" and chill in the refrigerator for about 2 hours.

CREMA DI ZUPPA INGLESE
SICILIAN TRIFLE

- **300** G / ¾ LB SPONGE CAKE
- **3** EGG WHITES
- **50** G / 2 OZ / ½ CUP CANDIED FRUIT, CUT UP
- **3** TBSP GRANULATED SUGAR CANDIED ORANGE PEEL
- **125** ML / 4 FL OZ / ½ CUP CONFECTIONER'S CUSTARD (SEE FOLLOWING RECIPE)
- **60** ML / 2 FL OZ / 4 TBSP ALCHERMES OR CHERRY BRANDY
- **60** ML / 2 FL OZ / 4 TBSP RUM

PREPARATION TIME: 1½ HOURS

SLICE THE SPONGE CAKE. Pour the confectioner's custard into a bowl (reserving 3-4 tablespoonsful) and add the candied fruit, cut to pieces. Transfer the reserved custard to a deep oven dish and arrange half the sponge cake slices (sprinkled with the red liqueur) on top. Cover with the candied fruit and confectioner's custard and then the remaining sponge cake slices, sprinkled with the rum. Whisk the egg whites until stiff, add 2 tablespoons sugar and pour over the trifle.

Decorate the surface with the candied orange peel, dredge with sugar and bake in a moderate oven until the meringue has dried out.

CREMA FRITTA O LATTE FRITTO

FRIED CUSTARD

◆

- 120 G / 5 OZ / SCANT CUP CORNFLOUR (CORNSTARCH)
- 1 L / 2 PTS / 4 CUPS MILK
- 4 EGGS, SEPARATED
- WHITE FLOUR
- DRY BREADCRUMBS
- ICING (CONFECTIONERS') SUGAR
- OIL

◆

PREPARATION TIME: 1 HOUR

PUT THE EGG YOLKS with the cornflour and sugar in a saucepan, add the milk and stir well to dissolve the cornflour. Transfer the pan over a flame and keep stirring in the same direction until the custard has thickened.

As soon as it starts to boil, draw off the heat and pour the custard onto a dampened marble slab or a large, moistened ceramics plate. When it has cooled off, cut into small fingers, roll in flour, in the whisked egg white and in the breadcrumbs. Fry in hot oil. Dredge with icing sugar and serve.

CREMA PASTICCERA

CONFECTIONER'S CUSTARD

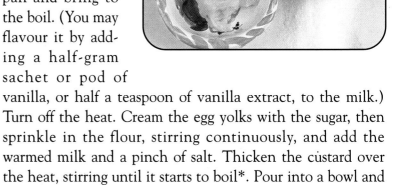

◆

- 4 EGG YOLKS
- 100 G / 4 OZ / ½ CUP GRANULATED SUGAR
- 50 G / 2 OZ / ⅓ CUP WHITE FLOUR
- ½ L / 1 PT / 2 CUPS MILK
- PINCH SALT

◆

PREPARATION TIME: 1 HOUR

POUR THE MILK into a pan and bring to the boil. (You may flavour it by adding a half-gram sachet or pod of vanilla, or half a teaspoon of vanilla extract, to the milk.) Turn off the heat. Cream the egg yolks with the sugar, then sprinkle in the flour, stirring continuously, and add the warmed milk and a pinch of salt. Thicken the custard over the heat, stirring until it starts to boil*. Pour into a bowl and leave to cool. This custard can be used as a filling for cream puffs, for short pastry or flaky pastry pies, for "iris", etc.

———————

*THE MILK found in the shops nowadays is pasteurised and therefore merely heating it up is enough.

CUCCÌA
WHEAT CAKE

- 1 KG / 2 LBS / 12 CUPS CRACKED WHEAT
- 150 G / 6 OZ / 1 CUP CORNFLOUR (CORN STARCH)
- 2 L / 4 PTS / 8 CUPS MILK
- 400 G / 14 OZ / 2 CUPS GRANULATED SUGAR
- 80 G / 3 OZ / ⅜ CUP CANDIED PUMPKIN
- 150 G / 6 OZ / ¾ CUP PLAIN (SEMI-SWEET) CHOCOLATE
- 1 LEMON
- CHERRIES IN SYRUP
- FEW SLICES ORANGES IN SYRUP

PREPARATION TIME: 1 HOUR, PLUS 3 DAYS FOR SOAKING THE WHEAT

LEAVE THE WHEAT to soak for 3 days, changing the water every day. Drain. Dissolve the cornflour in the milk and add the grated lemon rind. Put the milk and cornflour in a saucepan and cook over low heat, stirring assiduously. As soon as the liquid becomes creamy, draw off the heat and pour in the wheat. Cool and add the chocolate and candied pumpkin in pieces. Turn into a large platter and garnish with the cherries and oranges.

VARIATION: "cuccìa" can be made with 1 kg (2 lbs / 5½ cups) ricotta cheese prepared as for the "cannoli" filling.

FRITTELLE DI CARNEVALE
CARNIVAL FRITTERS

- ¾ L / 1½ PTS / 3 CUPS MILK
- ¼ L / ½ PT / 1 CUP WATER
- 20 G / ¾ OZ / 1½ TBSP FRESH BREWER'S YEAST
- 2 TBSP OLIVE OIL
- 50 G / 2 OZ / ¼ CUP GRANULATED SUGAR
- 2 WHISKED EGGS
- 100 G / 4 OZ / ⅔ CUP RAISINS
- FRESHLY GRATED ZEST OF 1 ORANGE
- 1 TBSP HONEY
- 40 G / 1½ OZ / ⅓ CUP WHITE FLOUR
- CINNAMON

PREPARATION TIME: 3 HOURS

HEAT THE MILK AND WATER for a very few minutes and dissolve the brewer's yeast in it. Add the oil, the sugar and the whisked eggs. Sprinkle in the flour, stirring slowly so that lumps do not form. When you have a nice, thick cream, add the raisins and the slightly-floured orange rind. Stir well and cover with the lid. Wrap the saucepan in a woollen cloth. When the batter is well risen after about an hour, drop spoonfuls into plenty of hot oil and fry. Dissolve a tablespoon of honey in a little water in a small pan, dip the fritters into the honeyed water, dust with sugar and cinnamon and eat hot.

FRITTELLE DI RICOTTA
RICOTTA CHEESE FRITTERS

◆

- 200 G / 8 OZ / 1 GENEROUS CUP RICOTTA CHEESE
- 200 G / 8 OZ / 1⅓ CUPS WHITE FLOUR
- 2 EGGS
- GRATED ZEST OF 1 LEMON
- PINCH SALT
- 1 TBSP HONEY
- CINNAMON
- OIL FOR FRYING

◆

PREPARATION TIME: 3 HOURS

WORK THE RICOTTA with the flour, eggs, a pinch of cinnamon and the grated lemon zest. Leave to rest for a couple of hours. Put a little of the mixture in the palm of your hand and shape into little rings. Deep fry them in a frying pan with plenty of hot oil. Dissolve a tablespoonful of honey in 60 ml (4 tbsp) water in a small pan and pour over the ricotta fritters. Dust with sugar and cinnamon.

THE DOUGH used in this recipe is not leavened. The fritters therefore will be flat, not puffed up like in the previous recipe.

IRIS

FRIED RICOTTA PUFFS

◆

- 500 G / 1 LB / 3½ CUPS WHITE FLOUR
- 30 G / 1 OZ / 2 TBSP FRESH BREWER'S YEAST
- ½ L / 1 PT / 2 CUPS MILK
- 1 EGG
- 50 G / 2 OZ / 4 TBSP LARD, BUTTER OR OIL
- 400 G / 14 OZ / 2¼ CUPS RICOTTA CHEESE
- 200 G / 8 OZ / 1 CUP GRANULATED SUGAR
- 100 G / 4 OZ / ½ CUP PLAIN (SEMI-SWEET) CHOCOLATE
- 100 G / 4 OZ / ½ CUP CANDIED PUMPKIN
- 2 EGGS
- DRY BREADCRUMBS
- OIL

◆

PREPARATION TIME: 3 HOURS

KNEAD THE FLOUR with the lard, eggs, brewer's yeast dissolved in a little warm milk, the remaining milk and a quarter of the sugar. Work the dough until soft, cover and leave to rise for about two hours. Meanwhile, prepare the filling by putting the ricotta with the rest of the sugar in a bowl. Mash with a fork until you have a smooth cream. You may add a little milk if the ricotta is rather thick. Add the chocolate and candied pumpkin cut to pieces. When the dough has risen, roll it out with a rolling pin and cut out rounds with the rim of a glass. In the centre of each ring put a spoonful of cream and seal with another round on top. Prove for another hour. When the iris are nice and puffy, dip them into beaten egg and then dry breadcrumbs and fry them in boiling oil in a deep pan.

145

MOSTACCIOLI

RICH FRUIT TART

◆

FOR THE PASTRY:

- 400G / 14OZ / 2²/3 CUPS PLAIN FLOUR
- 150G / 5OZ / 3/4 CUP GRANULATED SUGAR
- 2 EGGS
- MILK
- 100G / 4OZ / 1/2 CUP LARD

FOR THE FILLING:

- 100G / 4OZ / 1/2 CUP HONEY
- ALMONDS AND HAZELNUTS, TOASTED
- WALNUT KERNELS
- HALF AN ORANGE
- PLAIN FLOUR
- GROUND CINNAMON

◆

PREPARATION: 1 HOUR AND 40 MINUTES

PILE THE FLOUR INTO A HEAP ON A PASTRY BOARD and work in half a glass (1/4 cup) of milk.

Make a smooth dough with the sugar, 80g (3oz/6 tbs.) lard and the eggs.

Roll into a ball and allow it to rest for half-an-hour.

Dilute the honey in half a glass of water and pour into a small pan.

Bring to the boil and gradually sprinkle in a tablespoon of flour, one handful of chopped almonds and one of chopped hazelnuts, a handful of walnut kernels, grated orange rind and a pinch of cinnamon.

Roll out the dough into a fairly thin sheet.

Cut into 4- by 2-inch rectangles. At the centre of each, place a mound of the filling, and wrap the pastry diagonally around itself.

Lay the mustazzola in an oven dish greased with lard and place in a pre-heated oven at 200 °C / 400 °F / Gas Mark 6 for about half an hour.

MANDORLE GLASSATE
ICED ALMONDS

- 300 G / ¾ LB SHELLED ALMONDS
- 1 EGG WHITE
- 150 G / 6 OZ / 1⅛ CUP ICING (CONFECTIONERS') SUGAR
- 60 ML / 2 FL OZ / ¼ CUP WATER

PREPARATION TIME: 30 MINUTES

TOAST THE ALMONDS in a hot oven for five minutes. Whisk the egg whites until stiff, fold in the sugar, the water and the nuts. Stir well and leave to cool.

VARIATION: you may flavour the glacé icing (frosting) by replacing the plain water with: jasmine-flavoured water, vanilla dissolved in water, or the juice of one lemon.

PAN DI SPAGNA
SPONGE CAKE

- ■ 250 G / ½ LB / 1¼ CUPS GRANULATED SUGAR
- ■ 100 G / 4 OZ / ⅔ CUP WHITE FLOUR
- ■ 100 G / 4 OZ / ¾ CUP CORNFLOUR (CORNSTARCH)
- ■ 8 EGGS
- ■ 1 TBSP LARD OR BUTTER
- ■ PINCH SALT
- ■ GRATED LEMON ZEST

PREPARATION TIME: 1 HOUR

CREAM TOGETHER THE YOLKS AND SUGAR until soft and frothy. Slowly add the flour, salt and grated lemon zest. Whisk the egg whites until stiff. Cook the creamed yolks in a "bain-marie" (the water must not boil) and gradually fold in the egg whites, sprinkling the cornflour over and adding the melted lard or butter in a thin stream. When everything is well blended, pour into a deep baking tin or dish (8-10in. diameter) which has been oiled and floured. Bake in a moderate oven for 30-40 minutes.

PASTA FRITTA CON MIELE
FRIED LOAVES WITH HONEY

◆

- 1 KG / 2 LBS LEAVENED DOUGH
- 1 TBSP HONEY
- PINCH CINNAMON
- 1 TBSP GRANULATED SUGAR
- OLIVE OIL

◆

PREPARATION TIME: 30 MINUTES

KNEAD THE LEAVENED DOUGH with a tablespoon of oil. Make little flat loaves and fry in hot oil. Place the little loaves on a large serving dish and pour over the honey dissolved in 60 ml (4 tbsp) water.

Dredge with sugar and cinnamon and eat while hot.

THIS DISH has almost disappeared because bread is rarely made at home nowadays.

In Italy, bakers will sell leavened dough across the counter, so half your work is done!

PIGNUCCATA
FRIED PASTRY

◆

- **500** G / **1** LB / **3½** CUPS FLOUR
- **5** EGG YOLKS
- **200** G / **8** OZ / **1** CUP HONEY
- **50** G / **2** OZ / ¼ CUP GRANULATED SUGAR
- **60** ML / **2** FL OZ / ¼ CUP WATER OR ORANGE WATER
- GRATED ZEST OF **1** ORANGE OR LEMON
- PINCH SALT
- PINCH CINNAMON
- VEGETABLE OIL OR LARD FOR FRYING
- ICING (CONFECTIONERS') SUGAR

◆

PREPARATION TIME: 1 HOUR

HEAP THE FLOUR UP on a work surface and pour the yolks, a pinch of salt and the sugar into a hollow in the middle. Knead to a soft, even dough.

Form into fingers of the thickness of breadsticks, cut into small lengths and fry in boiling lard or vegetable oil.

In a small pan, dissolve the honey in the plain or flavoured water with the grated lemon or orange zest. Pile the fried pastries into a pyramid or pine cone (this is where the name comes from) on a serving dish. Dust with icing sugar and cinnamon.

In the Messina district, "pignuccata" is typically served covered with cocoa and lemon icing (frosting).

Ravioli dolci

Sweet Ravioli

FOR THE PASTRY:

- 500G / 1LB2OZ / 31/3 CUP PLAIN FLOUR
- 100G / 4OZ / 1/2 CUP GRANULATED SUGAR
- 80G / 3OZ / 6 TBSP LARD (OR BUTTER)
- 1 EGG YOLK
- VANILLA ESSENCE
- ICING (CONFECTIONER'S) SUGAR - FOR DECORATING
- OIL FOR FRYING
  FOR THE FILLING
- 450G / 1LB / 21/4 CUPS FRESH RICOTTA CHEESE
- 120G / 5OZ / 5/8 CUP GRANULATED SUGAR
- VANILLA ESSENCE
- HALF A LEMON
- GROUND CINNAMON
- CANDIED PUMPKIN
- PLAIN (SEMI-SWEET) CHOCOLATE (HALF A BAR)

♦

PREPARATION: 2 HOURS

MIX THE FLOUR WITH HALF A GLASS OF WATER, working in the sugar, the lard, the beaten egg yolk and a drop of vanilla essence.

When the dough is smooth and elastic, form it into a ball and leave for half an hour to rest.

To make the filling, use a spatula to combine the sugar, grated lemon rind, a drop of vanilla essence, a pinch of cinnamon, a tablespoon of diced candied pumpkin and the crumbled chocolate with the ricotta. Blend well.

Roll out the pastry thinly and cut into 6-inch squares.

Pile a little of the filling to one side of each square, fold the other side over and trim the edges with the special instrument for making ravioli.

Fry the pastry squares in plenty of boiling oil.

When they have turned golden, drain them and dredge with icing (confectioner's) sugar.

SENI DI VERGINE

CANDIED FRUIT CUSTARD TARTS

◆

- 400G / 14OZ / 22/3 CUPS PLAIN FLOUR
- 150G / 5OZ / 3/4 CUP GRANULATED SUGAR
- 150G / 5OZ / 3/4 CUP LARD
- CONFECTIONER'S CUSTARD (SEE BELOW)
- 1 EGG
- MILK
- CANDIED PUMPKIN
- PLAIN (SEMI-SWEET) CHOCOLATE (HALF A BAR)
- ICING (CONFECTIONER'S) SUGAR, TO DECORATE

◆

PREPARATION: 2 HOURS AND 20 MINUTES

MIX THE FLOUR INTO THE MILK (about a glass or half a cup) along with the sugar and the lard, until you have a smooth, fluid dough.

Form a ball and leave an hour to rest.

Roll out the dough into two differently-sized sheets.

At regular intervals, place spoonfuls of confectioner's custard, mixed with cubes of candied pumpkin (a tablespoon) and the chocolate in pieces, on the smaller one.

With beaten egg yolk, brush the pastry all round the mounds of filling.

Lay the other sheet of pastry on top and seal the edges.

Use a small, round, scalloped mould to cut out the tarts.

Brush each one with stiffly-whisked egg white and bake in a pre-heated oven at 200 °C / 400 °F / Gas Mark 6 for 20 minutes.

When the pastries are cooked, dust them with icing (confectioner's) sugar.

TO MAKE THE CONFECTIONER'S CUSTARD, slowly bring half a litre (1 pint / 21/2 cups) of milk to boiling point with 70g (3oz / 6 tbs.) granulated sugar, some lemon rind and a drop of vanilla essence in a milkpan. Meanwhile beat 4 egg yolks with 60g (2oz / 3/8 cup) granulated sugar, gradually folding in 2 tablespoons flour. Dilute the mixture with a drop of boiling milk and add to the pan. Thicken for 10-12 minutes over gentle heat, stirring with a whisk.

SFINCI DI SAN GIUSEPPE
ST JOSEPH CREAM PUFFS

◆

- 150 G / 6 FL OZ / ¾ CUP WATER
- 100 G / 4 OZ / ⅔ CUP WHITE FLOUR
- 3 EGGS
- 100 G / 4 OZ / ¾ CUP ICING (CONFECTIONERS') SUGAR
- SACHET / ¼ TSP VANILLA POWDER / ½ TSP VANILLA EXTRACT
- 1 TBSP COGNAC
- 2 TBSP LARD OR 50 G / 2 OZ / 4 TBSP BUTTER
- GRATED ZEST OF 1 LEMON
- PINCH SALT
- OIL

THE FILLING:
- 500 G / 1 LB / 2¾ CUPS RICOTTA CHEESE
- 250 G / ½ LB / 1¼ CUPS GRANULATED SUGAR
- 100 G / 4 OZ / ½ CUP PLAIN (SEMI-SWEET) CHOCOLATE, DICED
- 50 G / 2 OZ / ¼ CUP CANDIED FRUIT
- 25 G / 1 OZ / 2 TBSP CANDIED ORANGE PEEL
- 25 G / 1 OZ / 2 TBSP PISTACHIOS, CHOPPED

◆

PREPARATION TIME: 3 HOURS

BRING THE WATER to the boil with the fat and salt, then throw in the flour, stirring well until thoroughly cooked (about 10 minutes). Remove the dough and spread it out over a work surface to cool rapidly. When cold, work in one egg yolk, add one stiffly-whisked egg white and, with a wooden spoon, continue mixing until incorporated. Repeat the procedure with the other two eggs.

The end result should be smooth and creamy. Pour plenty of oil into a deep frying pan and, when boiling, spoon in the dough to obtain soft, even-sized fritters. Once fried, allow to cool and slit each one open with a knife.

Meanwhile, work the ricotta into the icing sugar in a bowl and, if the mixture is too stiff, add a few drops of milk.

When the mixture is nice and creamy, add the chocolate and candied fruit.

Fill the cold "sfinci" and garnish with candied orange peel and the chopped pistachios.

156

TESTA DI TURCO
FRIED PASTRY WITH CHOCOLATE CUSTARD

- 150 G / 6 OZ / 1 CUP WHITE FLOUR
- 25 G / 1 TBSP BITTER COCOA
- 1 TBSP LARD OR BUTTER
- 1 EGG
- 1 TBSP GRANULATED SUGAR
- 50 G / 2 OZ / ¼ CUP RED WINE OR MARSALA
- PINCH SALT
- OIL FOR FRYING
- 1 L / 2 PTS / 4 CUPS MILK
- 100 G / 4 OZ / ¾ CUP CORNFLOUR (CORNSTARCH)
- 100 G / 4 OZ / ½ CUP GRANULATED SUGAR
- PINCH CINNAMON
- 100 G / 4 OZ PLAIN (SEMI-SWEET) CHOCOLATE, DICED
- 50 G / 2 OZ / 2 TBSP BITTER COCOA
- GRATED ZEST OF 1 LEMON
- 1 SACHET / ¼ TSP VANILLA POWDER / ½ TSP VANILLA EXTRACT (OPTIONAL)

PREPARATION TIME: 4 HOURS

KNEAD THE FLOUR, egg, the cocoa dissolved in the Marsala or wine, the fat and the sugar into a smooth paste. Leave to rest in a cool place (or in the refrigerator) for a few hours. Roll out the dough into a thin sheet, cut into rectangles and fry them in hot oil. Dry on kitchen paper.

Prepare a cream by putting the cornflour, cocoa and sugar in a saucepan and dissolving it all in the cold milk, as you add some little by little to prevent lumps from forming.

Sprinkle in the grated lemon zest and the vanilla. Bring gently to the boil over medium heat, stirring continuously, then draw off the heat immediately.

Put a layer of the fried pastry in a deep bowl and pour a little of the cream over. Repeat the layers until all the ingredients have been used up. Dredge the top layer with cocoa and scatter pieces of plain chocolate over.

Chill in the refrigerator for a few hours before serving.

157

TORRONCINI

NOUGAT

◆

- 500 G / 1 LB / 2½ CUPS GRANULATED SUGAR
- 250 G / ½ LB / 2½ CUPS ALMONDS, TOASTED AND CHOPPED
- 250 G / ½ LB / 2½ CUPS PISTACHIOS, CHOPPED
- 50 G / 2 OZ / ¼ CUP HONEY ALMOND OR VEGETABLE OIL

◆

PREPARATION TIME: 1 HOUR

DISSOLVE THE SUGAR with the honey in a saucepan and add the almonds and pistachios. Cook for 5-10 minutes over a slow heat to allow the flavours to blend. Pour onto a slab of oiled marble (preferably with almond oil), spread it out with a spatula and cut into short lengths. When the nougat is cold, wrap each piece in greaseproof (wax) paper and store in glass jars.

IN SICILY, nougat is not only made with almonds and pistachios, but there are also versions with peanuts or sesame seeds.

TORTA DI RISO
SWEET RICE PUDDING

- 200 G / 8 OZ / 1 CUP RICE
- ½ L / 1 PT / 2 CUPS MILK
- 100 G / 4 OZ / ½ CUP GRANULATED SUGAR
- 2 EGGS, SEPARATED
- GRATED ZEST OF 1 LEMON
- 50 G / 2 OZ / ⅓ CUP RAISINS
- 1 SACHET / ¼ TSP VANILLA POWDER / ½ TSP VANILLA EXTRACT (OPTIONAL)
- DRY BREADCRUMBS
- OIL

PREPARATION TIME: 3 HOURS (ONLY 40 MINUTES IF YOU COOK THE RICE A DAY AHEAD, ADDING THE EGG YOLKS THE FOLLOWING MORNING)

BOIL THE RICE for 5-6 minutes in salted water. Drain and continue cooking in another saucepan with the milk and a glass of water brought to the boil.

Add the sugar, the grated lemon zest and (if wished) the vanilla. When the rice is cooked, add the raisins tossed in flour, draw off the heat and allow to cool.

One at a time, incorporate the egg yolks into the rice, stirring well. Whisk the egg whites until stiff and fold into the mixture. Pour into an oiled-and-crumbed baking tin or dish and bake in a moderate oven for 30 minutes.

VARIATION: you can use the same mixture as a filling for a short pastry crust.